INTENTIONAL
TEACHING

To our students, who bring immeasurable joy to our lives. We seek to honor your efforts in the pursuit of self-discovery as learners. We humbly dedicate this book to you.

INTENTIONAL TEACHING

TEACHING

The **Let Me Learn**®Classroom in Action

BONNIE U. DAWKINS
ROBERT B. KOTTKAMP
CHRISTINE A. JOHNSTON

CORWIN
A SAGE Company

For information:

Corwin
A SAGE Company
2455 Teller Road
Thousand Oaks, California 91320
(800) 233-9936
Fax: (800) 417-2466
www.corwin.com

SAGE Ltd.
1 Oliver's Yard
55 City Road
London EC1Y 1SP
United Kingdom

SAGE Pvt. Ltd.
B 1/I 1 Mohan Cooperative
   Industrial Area
Mathura Road, New Delhi 110 044
India

SAGE Asia-Pacific Pte. Ltd.
33 Pekin Street #02-01
Far East Square
Singapore 048763

Printed in the United States of America

Library of Congress Cataloging-in-Publication Data

Dawkins, Bonnie U.
Intentional teaching : the let me learn classroom in action/Bonnie U. Dawkins, Robert B. Kottkamp, Christine A. Johnston.
      p. cm.
Includes bibliographical references and index.
ISBN 978-1-4129-5186-9 (pbk. : alk. paper)
   1. Learning, Psychology of. 2. Teaching—Psychological aspects. 3. Brain.
I. Kottkamp, Robert B. II. Johnston, Christine A. III. Title.

LB1060.D386 2010
371.39—dc22   2010003017

This book is printed on acid-free paper.

10 11 12 13 14 10 9 8 7 6 5 4 3 2 1

Acquisitions Editor:	Carol Chambers Collins
Associate Editor:	Megan Bedell
Editorial Assistant:	Sarah Bartlett
Production Editor:	Veronica Stapleton
Copy Editor:	Codi Bowman
Typesetter:	C&M Digitals (P) Ltd.
Proofreader:	Jennifer Gritt
Indexer:	Sheila Bodell
Cover Designer:	Rose Storey
Figure Designer:	Priscilla Jeschke

Contents

List of Figures

Chapter 6

Chapter 7

Appendix

Preface

For over a decade, between 1994 and 2009, Christine Johnston along with teachers and administrators at 19 national and international sites—including faculty at the University of Malta; Queens University, Belfast; St. Johns York University, UK; University of Tarragona, Spain; Hofstra and Adelphi Universities, NY, and the University of South Florida—worked with and assessed the Learning Connections Inventory (LCI): the instrument used to launch the Let Me Learn (LML) Process. Gathering results from more than 15,000 6- through 18-year-old students (including regular education, special education, dispraxic/neurologically impaired students, and Westinghouse National Science Scholars) and 7,000 adult professionals, researchers from these institutions have directed a research agenda that has established the validity and reliability of the LCI and the LML process in K–16 faculty and staff development and corporate human resource training (Borg & Calleja, 2006; Buchanan, 2005; Calleja, 1998; Campbell, 2005; C. Johnston, 2005, 2006; Kottkamp & Silverberg, 2006; Marcellino, 2001; McSweeney, 2005; Osterman & Kottkamp, 2004; Silverberg, 2002). *The Learning Combinations Inventory Manual* (C. Johnston & Dainton, 1997, 2004) contains the original studies of validity and reliability (Addy, 1996; Borg, 1996; Hayes, 1996; C. Johnston, 1996; J. Johnston, 1996; Mifsud, 1996).

The book came about as the natural coalescing of Chris, Bob, and Bonnie's related research agendas on learning. Chris and Bob have worked together from 1982 until present beginning with Bob chairing her dissertation on professional communication. In a reversed teacher/student role set, Bob became Chris's trusted colleague as LML concepts and tools were developed and tested in varied contexts: the Republic of Malta's education system; a California community college; a small DuPont plant in Rochester, NY; accelerated LML professional development courses, and national conferences. Bob has served on LML's advisory board since its inception.

Bonnie Dawkins began her educational leadership doctoral education in 2000 at Hofstra University where Bob introduced her to LML research resulting in Bonnie asking him to chair her dissertation. Bonnie chose to study implementing LML in her classroom. The segue, from research dissertation to educator friendly book and from hierarchical to collegial interaction among the authors, resulted in *Intentional Teaching* and a great deal of fun in the process.

Acknowledgments

The collaboration in creating this book has been extraordinarily dynamic. Steeped in trust and rooted firmly in the belief the Let Me Learn (LML) Process provides the ideas and tools for building learner capacity, we have worked to bring life to these stories and insights from the classroom. We hope *Intentional Teaching: The Let Me Learn Classroom in Action* will enable educators to make the learner truly central in schools.

We are grateful to our colleagues, friends, and family members who have supported us throughout this endeavor. They provided the sanctuary required for us to engage in sustained inquiry, reflection, analysis, and writing.

We are exceptionally indebted to LML extended family members who read an early draft and provided honest response on where we got it right and where we got it wrong. Jackie Anderson, Chris Bloom, Donna Jorgensen, Christine Laspata, and Melissa Smith, we gratefully acknowledge your fidelity to us as learners and to the future of LML. We thank Joel Johnston for 11th-hour editing and formatting.

Our greatest appreciation is extended to the learners in Bonnie's classroom during her implementation year. Though we may recognize them, necessarily, only through pseudonyms, they made this endeavor possible. These young learners through their daily lives and work of learning provided the story of challenge, struggle, joy, openness, and self-discovery. We attempt to illuminate this process for teachers and educators who intend to make learners and learning the actualized center of our educative efforts. We admire their courage to become more intentional learners and wish them continued growth and bright futures. Although only a few learner voices are represented directly, as a collective, they are all the heart of our efforts to make the learning process transparent and accessible.

Bonnie, Bob, and Chris

Publisher's Acknowledgments

Corwin Press gratefully acknowledges the contributions of the following individuals:

Patti Grammens, Teacher
South Forsyth Middle School
Cumming, Georgia

Holly Johnson, Associate Professor
University of Cincinnati, Teacher Education
Cincinnati, Ohio

Thea H. Williams-Black, Assistant Professor of Elementary
   Education
The University of Mississippi
Oxford, Mississippi

Robert E. Yager, Professor of Science Education
University of Iowa
Iowa City, Iowa

About the Authors

 **Dr. Bonnie U. Dawkins** is an elementary school teacher with 25 years experience in public education. She received her EdD from Hofstra University in 2008, her EdM from Harvard University, and her BA from The Catholic University of America. Dr. Dawkins is lead teacher in her school and regularly conducts professional development workshops on learning, teaching, and curriculum. Her research interests include reflective practice and teacher and student learning. Her certification in the Let Me Learn (LML) Process equips her as an LML consultant and mentor.

 **Dr. Robert B. Kottkamp** is professor emeritus, Department of Foundations, Leadership and Policy Studies, Hofstra University. He received his BA from DePauw University and both MAEd and PhD from Washington University. Dr. Kottkamp has coauthored five books, the latest being *Reflective Practice for Educators: Professional Development to Improve Student Learning* (Second Edition) with Karen F. Osterman. His chapter with Edith A. Rusch, The Landscape of Scholarship on the Education of School Leaders, 1985–2006, recently appeared in the *Handbook of Research on the Education of School Leaders* (2009). He maintains a keen interest in the continuing development of the LML Process and in researching its processes and effects. Professor Kottkamp is fortunate to have chaired the doctoral research of coauthors Dr. Chris Johnston and Dr. Bonnie Dawkins; creating this book together as peers has been a wonderfully fulfilling learning experience.

 **Christine A. Johnston** is the former director of the Center for the Advancement of Learning, Rowan University where she was the head of research inquiries studying the effects of the LML Process on teacher-student interaction, student learning outcomes, literacy, and student persistence. For the past 11 years, she has engaged in studies on the LML Process including work with 19 universities in the United States and abroad, and 38 U.S. school districts including a two-year consultancy to the EU's Grundtvig Project working with participants from Italy, Spain, the UK, the Czech Republic, Slovenia, Malta, and Holland. Dr. Johnston received her EdD from Rutgers University in 1985, her MA from the University of Wisconsin–Milwaukee, and her BA from the University of Wisconsin–Eau Claire. Dr. Johnston currently serves on the external advisory board to the University of Wisconsin–Eau Claire's College of Education and Human Sciences. She has authored and coauthored five books and numerous articles and chapters on the LML Process. She has been the recipient of a Ford Foundation Educational Internship; an NSF Graduate Fellowship; a Department of Education, State of New Jersey, education-innovation grant; and a Corporate DuPont Education grant.

Introduction

Learning: The Center of the Educational Universe

This is a book about learning and the journey of one teacher, Bonnie Dawkins, who sought to make an intentional change in her teaching through implementing the Let Me Learn (LML) System in her classroom. Bonnie's experiences and those of her students recounted in this book are taken from a research base (Dawkins, 2008), as are the theory and processes of *Let Me Learn* (C. Johnston, 1996). However, this book translates those research bases into an educator friendly style avoiding the feel of an "academic" text while providing references for those who wish to dig more deeply.

Theme and Context

Why the focus on learning? In the context of current education in the United States, learning is *assumed* central to the enterprise. Assumed is the operative word. By comparison to curriculum, teaching, standards, and assessment—all of which stress content—the *process* of learning is little addressed and little understood. The typical title for the academic departments that prepare teachers remains: curriculum and instruction. Attempts to raise scores on high-stakes state tests typically emphasize content and teaching techniques: not learning, not student learning, and not teacher learning.

The authors of this book make learning explicit and central, rather than assumed, because improving our schools and their outcomes will not occur without concentrated focus on what is the under-attended foundation of all educative efforts.

Our Lens: The Let Me Learn System

We believe the path that leads to Intentional Teaching begins by addressing learning through the theory, processes, lexicon, and tools of LML, an Advanced Learning System (C. Johnston, 2000). Using this Advanced Learning System, teachers and learners first come to understand their unique approaches to learning and then the unique approaches used by others, be they teacher or student. Using LML concepts and tools, learners decode learning tasks and compare what the task requires to their approach to learning. When there is a mismatch, learners develop strategies to guide a more intentional approach to accomplishing the task. The upshot is that learners come to control and regulate their learning through knowing themselves as learners as well as those with whom they collaborate to complete a learning task. When LML was first introduced to educators 15 years ago, it was sometimes misperceived as another explanation of learning akin to learning styles, multiple intelligences, and the like, However, those who used it with integrity soon realized that it was not a learning styles knock-off. The Let Me Learn Process is, instead, an integrated system that brings learning under the control of each individual learner, something the other approaches fail to do.

How the Book Is Organized

The first chapter presents a comprehensive description of the LML Advanced Learning System. Chapter 2 introduces Bonnie Dawkins as a teacher-learner and gives her perspective on the LML system and its impact. The remaining chapters, which correspond to the months of the school year, are a matrix of overlapping elements.

Each month/chapter begins with a vignette from Bonnie's direct experience, which captures an important experience or milestone in implementation and change. Then comes Bonnie's reflection on the vignette followed by implementation activities, examples of lesson plans, materials, and activities Bonnie used in integrating LML implementation into her ongoing curriculum.

Vignettes

The vignettes in each chapter present Bonnie's direct experiences, in the situation and in first person. These descriptions take the reader into the classroom in real time. Some vignettes are milestones; they indicate major turning points in thinking or implementation of LML for Bonnie, for her students, or for both.

Months

Although the LML implementation process runs across the school year, months of the school calendar provide a way of dividing the implementation into segments that correspond to the way teachers often think and feel about particular time spans during the year. This organizing principle assures that the reader experiences a chronological progression of important events and emotional responses.

In tracking Bonnie's implementation experience, the September/ October chapter describes her introduction of the LML Process to students. From November through June, the chapters describe her integration of LML into her normal sixth-grade language arts curriculum and its regular classroom activities. It is in the second set of months that we see the embedding of LML into the traditional curriculum and how that changes the experiences of children and their teacher.

Voices

You will hear three different voices as you read this book, in addition to those of many students. The first voice is that of Bonnie Dawkins, the teacher-learner. Bonnie's voice begins each chapter, relating the vignettes that are taken directly from the copious field notes she wrote up every evening through the whole academic year of LML implementation. In doing the research that grounds this book, she took the position of participant observer: She was simultaneously fulfilling her role as sixth-grade teacher and acting as a researcher observing and recording data about her students and her thoughts, actions, and emotions. The reflective analysis following each vignette is also in Bonnie's voice. She describes not only what was going on in the classroom with her students but also the deep thoughts and feelings that she experienced while implementing a major change in her teaching and in herself as teacher-learner.

The second voice is that of Robert Kottkamp, who introduced Bonnie to the LML Process at Hofstra University through his classes and research. Sections with the subtitle of Bob's Perspective provide context, interpretation, larger perspective, and research grounding.

The third voice is that of Christine Johnston, originator of LML and its head researcher. Her voice is dominant in several chapters as well as the appendices, which together provide a detailed description of the LML Advanced Learning System. In the central classroom chapters, her voice is present in its editorial influence.

Finally, you will also hear from Bonnie's students, who number 62. They figure prominently in most vignettes, and they appear elsewhere as she refers to specific events and in some of the implementation activities. While not every student's voice is heard, the distribution of student-learner voices includes a wide variation in learning approaches and experiences. Student voices are typically in first person.

Who Should Read This Book?

Whether you know anything about the LML Process or you are new to the concept and its effects, this book stands as a guide to implementing new approaches within your classroom. The questions posed at the end of each chapter will prompt reflection on the change that you observe within you and your classroom. The questions each chapter raises are especially effective if you are considering the implementation of the LML Process and hesitate because you want to know if you are doing it with fidelity. *Intentional Teaching* will set aside your fears and send you on a rich and insightful journey that could well change the course of your professional teaching life. *Intentional Teaching* honors teachers, professional development, and the focus of every classroom, by honoring the learners themselves and their capacity to learn, grow, and change.

1

What Is the Let Me Learn Advanced Learning System?

Learning is crucial to our existence. This perspective is not original or limited to the present-day. Centuries ago, ancient literature characterized learning as the wellspring of our existence. However, as the ancient literature explains, for learning to be maximized it needs to be used with intention. The learner needs to know and understand that learning encompasses the ability to think and reason, the motivation to engage and act, and the courage to acknowledge feelings and empathize. Any explanation of learning that seeks acceptance as authentic needs to acknowledge and reverence these points. Few explanations of learning meet this standard. One explanation that does is the Let Me Learn (LML) Process.

The inception of the LML Process began more than 15 years ago, when a group of academic researchers and educational practitioners sought to understand the source and potential of Intentional Learning. Their exploration and experimentation resulted in a science-based, learner-friendly explanation of learning, including the brain-mind connection, the Mental Processes it requires, and the potential it holds for individuals to use it with intention.

During the development of the LML Process, important insights into Intentional Learning yielded the development of a unique set of learning tools, an array of practical skills, and a set of terms to equip learners of all ages to communicate with others about their individual

Learning Processes. With the addition of these tools, skills, and a lexicon of learning terms, the designation of the LML Process expanded to include the phrase "an Advanced Learning System."

The Theoretical Basis for the Let Me Learn Process

How We Take in the World

The LML Process defines learning as "taking in the world around you and making sense of it" (C. Johnston, 2007). Although this is not a school-based definition of learning, it is comprehensive and at the same time parsimonious. This definition fits well with the rationale for why learning is vital to living. To survive and thrive, individuals need to be able to comprehend the world around them, interpret its effects on them, and determine how best to respond.

Understanding the brain-mind connection is the first step in understanding how learning occurs. Simply stated, the process of learning begins as the brain takes in stimuli through the five senses. Stimuli enter the brain in the form of sight, sound, taste, touch, and smell. Our sensory portals regulate the stimuli entering the brain. Once inside the brain, the stimuli are processed by neuroreceptors and electrochemicals using all sectors of the brain. However, the stimuli require translation, something to break the electrochemical and neuroreceptor codes. The interpreter-translator is found in the working memory of the mind. To reach the mind, the stimuli must pass through a brain-mind interface and enter the working memory where they are translated into symbolic representations (language, numbers, musical notes, scientific notation, and thousands of other symbols) to be stored and retrieved when needed (Bruer, 1994).

Patterns and the Brain–Mind Connection

The LML Process posits that the interface through which the stimuli pass consists of filters that sift the stimuli as they pass from the brain to the mind. The result of this sifting action yields functions hereafter referred to as Patterns of operation or Patterns. These Patterns are labeled Sequence, Precision, Technical Reasoning, and Confluence based on a factor analysis of their discrete operations. See Figure 1.1 for a graphic depiction of the fascinating process of the brain-mind connection.

Although these Patterns are universal across race, gender, and ethnicity, their makeup and use is very person-specific (Johnston & Dainton, 2004). All learners use all four Pattern filters but to varying

Figure 1.1 Representation of the Brain-Mind Connection

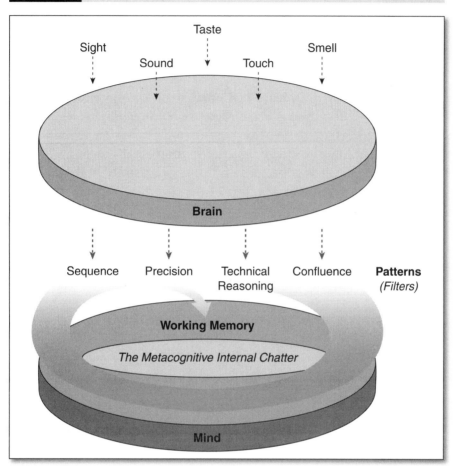

degrees. The degree to which we use each of these filters is measured by how each Pattern facilitates or limits the stimuli's entry into the mind. For example, a wide-open Pattern filter allows large amounts of specific stimuli to pass into the mind's translation and storage mechanism. However, a tightly closed Pattern filter may reject stimuli, seeking to Avoid having to cope with it.

Research indicates that most of us do not use *all Patterns* with equal comfort and naturalness (C. Johnston, 1996). We may use one or more of them to the maximum amount, one or more of them as needed—and we may do our best to Avoid one or more of them. The LML Process refers to these levels of use as Use First, Use As Needed, and Avoid. Whatever the degree to which these Patterns operate within each of us, the bottom line is the Patterns work as an internal team of processes when we engage in learning. Pattern scores are typically identified as four consecutive scale scores (i.e., S26 P19 T27 C20). Translated, these read Sequence (Use First), Precision (Use As Needed), Technical Reasoning (Use First at a level even higher than the use of Sequence), and Confluence (at the midpoint of Use As Needed). Throughout this text, the reader will encounter student and teacher scores written in this manner.

Yet another defining aspect of these Patterns is the internal working of each. Within each Pattern is found a set of Mental Processes, which are mentioned at the very start of this chapter: Cognition (the ability to think and reason), Conation (the motivation to engage and act), and Affectation (the courage to acknowledge feelings and to empathize). It is the interplay among your thoughts (Cognition), actions (Conation), and feelings (Affectation) that create a sense of comfort and wellbeing or discomfort and frustration within each Pattern. Figure 1.2 illustrates the nature of the interaction occurring among your thoughts, actions, and feelings within each Pattern.

Figure 1.2 Mental Processes That Operate Within Each Learning Pattern

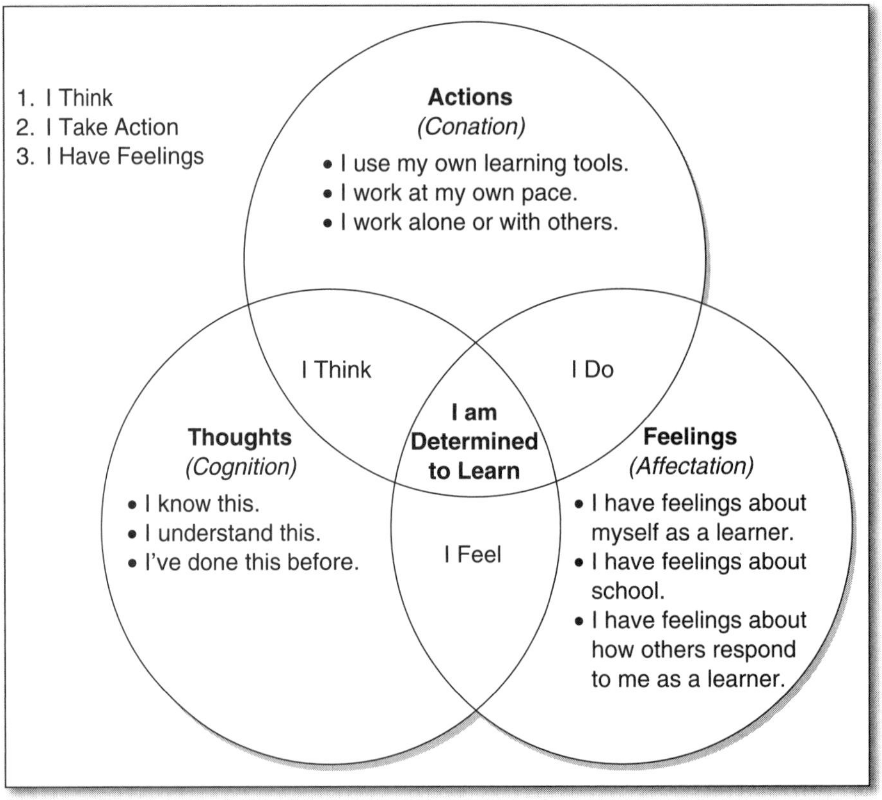

1. I Think
2. I Take Action
3. I Have Feelings

Actions
(Conation)
• I use my own learning tools.
• I work at my own pace.
• I work alone or with others.

I Think

I Do

I am Determined to Learn

Thoughts
(Cognition)
• I know this.
• I understand this.
• I've done this before.

I Feel

Feelings
(Affectation)
• I have feelings about myself as a learner.
• I have feelings about school.
• I have feelings about how others respond to me as a learner.

The First Tool: The Learning Connections Inventory

The instrument that launches the LML Advanced Learning System is the Learning Connections Inventory (LCI) (Johnston &

Dainton, 1997). The LCI is a self-administered "interview" that captures the degree to which an individual uses each of the four Patterns. Learners respond on a five-point scale to each of the LCI's 28 self-report items as shown in Figure 1.3. Learners also complete

Figure 1.3 Sample Items From the LCI Form II

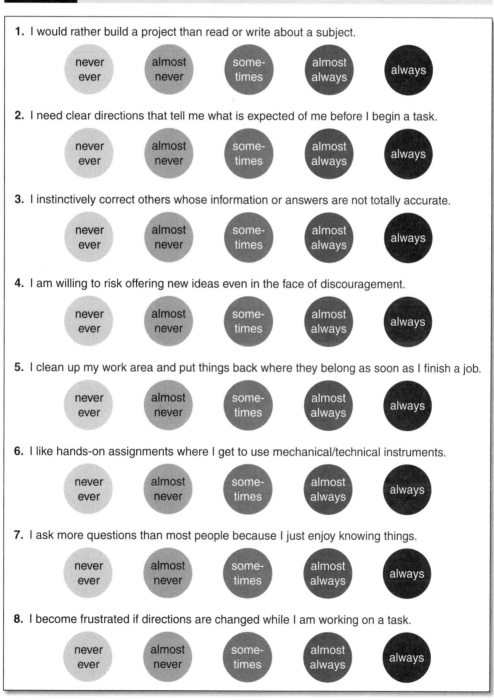

1. I would rather build a project than read or write about a subject.

   never ever · almost never · some-times · almost always · always

2. I need clear directions that tell me what is expected of me before I begin a task.

   never ever · almost never · some-times · almost always · always

3. I instinctively correct others whose information or answers are not totally accurate.

   never ever · almost never · some-times · almost always · always

4. I am willing to risk offering new ideas even in the face of discouragement.

   never ever · almost never · some-times · almost always · always

5. I clean up my work area and put things back where they belong as soon as I finish a job.

   never ever · almost never · some-times · almost always · always

6. I like hands-on assignments where I get to use mechanical/technical instruments.

   never ever · almost never · some-times · almost always · always

7. I ask more questions than most people because I just enjoy knowing things.

   never ever · almost never · some-times · almost always · always

8. I become frustrated if directions are changed while I am working on a task.

   never ever · almost never · some-times · almost always · always three short-answer, free-responses to questions such as, "What frustrates me most about completing an assignment is. . . ." There are no correct answers on the LCI, only what a person records as valid for him or her.

Tallying an individual's responses to the LCI produces a score for each of the four Learning Patterns (Figure 1.4). The individual's score for each Pattern falls into one of three ranges or levels: a score of 7 to 17 indicates Avoid, a score of 18 to 24 indicates Use As Needed, and a score of 25 to 35 indicates Use First (C. Johnston & Dainton, 2004).

Figure 1.4	Pattern Score Ranges or Levels for Learning Connections Inventory Patterns

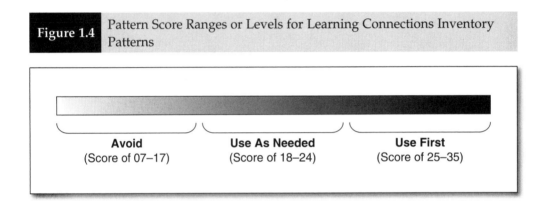

Avoid
(Score of 07–17)

Use As Needed
(Score of 18–24)

Use First
(Score of 25–35)

Responses to the short-answer questions are examined with a set of protocols that indicate the use of specific Learning Patterns. These responses are internal validity checks showing whether the individual's self-generated responses do or do not support the forced-choice answers. Additional data are used to validate LCI scores. These data include face-to-face discussions of scores, observations of learner behaviors, and examination of work products from varied learning tasks.

Student work product provides clear examples of student Pattern Combinations. Figure 1.5 shows exemplars of actual student work products collected by a vice-principal who observed the different Learning Patterns among members of her fifth-grade safety patrol. As you read the general description of each Learning Pattern, and the greater detail found in the Appendix, you may want to return to these visual representations of students' Pattern Combinations and note the specific Pattern characteristics found in each.

Figure 1.5	Safety Patrol Reports Indicating Pattern Differences

PATROL'S REPORT

Name: Stephen
Grade: 3 Teacher: Mrs. Hall

1. Hitting people with his bookbag

2. Saying swear-words

3. Pushing and shoving

4. Screaming

Patrol's name: Liam
Bus #: 412

S: 29   P: 21   T: 27   C: 20

PATROL'S REPORT

Name: Andrew
Grade: 1 Teacher: Watkins

Andrew was calling Mark a piece of shit and he was following what Derek was doing. I told him to stop but he just kept on going on saying it. He was just plugging his ears and sing lala but

Patrol's name: Amanda
Bus #: 9   he kept on saying it.

S: 25   P: 31   T: 34   C: 22

PATROL'S REPORT

Name: Jake
Grade: 3 Teacher: Ross

Fighting

Patrol's name: Adam
Bus #: 5

S: 21   P: 16   T: 27   C: 19

PATROL'S REPORT

Name: _____
Grade: ___ Teacher: _____

(No students using Confluence first had been selected for Safety Patrol!)

Patrol's name: _____
Bus #: ___

Understanding How Our Patterns Affect Our Learning

The first and most important LML skill involves understanding the depth and intricacies of each Pattern. Having developed this skill, you are able to understand fully the nature of the team of Patterns within you and, therefore, will be able to answer the overarching question, "How can I get my individualized team of Patterns to work well with one another for me to take in the world around me and make sense of it?" What follows are broad descriptions of each Pattern: For the specifics of the nature of thought, action, and feeling that typify each Pattern and what each score indicates about how an individual makes use of each Pattern, see Appendix Figures A.1–A.8, which explain each Pattern's spectrum from Use First to Avoid.

Sequence

I learn best when I have

- Clear, step-by-step directions
- Sufficient time to go over and over directions
- A sample to look at
- A plan to follow.

I say

- "What am I supposed to do?"
- "What do I do next?"
- "Could I see an example?"
- "Wait a minute! Don't go to the next one yet."

Precision

I learn best when I have

- A lot of detailed information
- Time to check if my work is correct
- Additional information to read
- An opportunity to ask many questions

I say

- "Is this right? What's the answer?"
- "Where can I find the answer?"
- "Well, actually..."
- "Wait a minute. I'm still writing."

Technical Reasoning

I learn best when I have

- Space to be left alone while working
- An opportunity to build things to show my skills
- An opportunity to learn from real-world experiences
- Hands-on projects instead of paper and pencil assignments

I say

- "When am I ever going to use this?"
- "I can do this myself!"
- "My homework? I didn't get it done."
- "Just let me put my head on my desk or sit here and play with my pencil."

Confluence

I learn best when I have

- The freedom to get started and ask for directions later
- The option to do assignments in a unique way
- An opportunity to take risks with new ideas
- A chance to learn from my failures

I say

- "Who will care if I do it differently?"
- "I've got another idea!"
- "I have lots of things started but not much finished!"
- "I love the word, 'imagine!'"

Different Pattern Combinations

It is useful to understand the effect of different levels of Pattern usage. Figure 1.6 provides examples of different types of Pattern Combinations which affect learners variously.

Dynamic

If you use one or two of your Patterns at the Use First level and any other combination of the remaining Patterns at Avoid or Use As Needed, you are a Dynamic Learner. You take in the world around you differently than those whose Patterns make them Bridge or Strong-willed Learners.

Bridge

If you don't Avoid any Patterns or use any at a Use First level, then you are a Bridge Learner. You learn from listening to others and interacting with them. You are comfortable using all of the Patterns. Sometimes you feel like a "jack-of-all-trades and a master of none," but you also find you can blend in, pitch in, and help make things happen as a contributing member of the group. You weigh things in the balance before you act. You lead from the middle by encouraging others rather than taking charge of the situation.

Strong-Willed

If you use three or more Patterns at the Use First level, you are a Strong-willed Learner. You are your own team. You prefer to work alone so that you can control the plan, the ideas, the talk, the decisions, the process, and the outcomes. Sometimes others find it hard to follow your lead (see Figure 1.6).

Figure 1.6 Dynamic, Bridge, and Strong-Willed Pattern Combinations

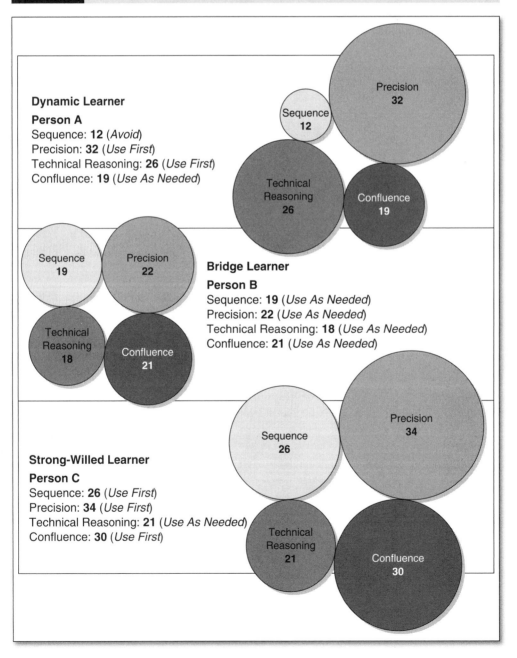

Dynamic Learner

Person A
Sequence: **12** (*Avoid*)
Precision: **32** (*Use First*)
Technical Reasoning: **26** (*Use First*)
Confluence: **19** (*Use As Needed*)

Sequence 12

Precision 32

Technical Reasoning 26

Confluence 19

Bridge Learner

Person B
Sequence: **19** (*Use As Needed*)
Precision: **22** (*Use As Needed*)
Technical Reasoning: **18** (*Use As Needed*)
Confluence: **21** (*Use As Needed*)

Sequence 19

Precision 22

Technical Reasoning 18

Confluence 21

Strong-Willed Learner

Person C
Sequence: **26** (*Use First*)
Precision: **34** (*Use First*)
Technical Reasoning: **21** (*Use As Needed*)
Confluence: **30** (*Use First*)

Sequence 26

Precision 34

Technical Reasoning 21

Confluence 30

The Second Tool: The Personal Learning Profile

The Personal Learning Profile is a record of your Learning Patterns described in your own words. It is a way of translating the Pattern scores into an authentic profile of you as a learner. It is your opportunity to personalize your Pattern descriptions by referring not just to the descriptive words and phrases from the Pattern descriptors but by including examples of how you experience your Patterns both in the classroom and outside.

Personalizing Your Pattern Description

The first step in the personalization of the Learning Patterns begins by reviewing the standard descriptors of each and identifying which of these describes you, the learner. After selecting the specific aspect, you convert the standard phrases into your personal phrases by recalling the words you typically use to describe your thinking, actions, and feelings when asked to complete a task that requires Sequence, Precision, Technical Reasoning, and Confluence as seen in Figure 1.7.

Figure 1.7 Personal Learning Profile

Example				For Your Profile			
	Use First	Use As Needed	Avoid		Use First	Use As Needed	Avoid
Sequence			9	Sequence			
Precision		21		Precision			
Technical Reasoning		19		Technical Reasoning			
Confluence	33			Confluence			
Explanation				Explanation			

Sequence

I am a person who Avoids directions. They just don't make sense to me. The most I can handle is a three-step process. After that, I prefer to figure it out on my own.

Sequence

Figure 1.7 (Continued)

Explanation	Explanation
Precision I use Precision as needed. Although I read a lot, I don't read nonfiction, factual books. I do research and dig into information when I am interested in a topic. I don't seek information just to know facts. I am not a walking almanac of minutia. **Technical Reasoning** I use my Technical Reasoning as needed, similar to my Precision. The part of Technical Reasoning that I relate to best is being able to work by myself. I am a loner not a joiner. I want just the right tool to get a job done, and I love gadgets, but I don't care how things work nor am I interested in fixing things. **Confluence** I use my Confluence as the leader of my personal learning team. I never met an idea I didn't like. If I do something once, the second time it becomes overworked and the third time boring. I like the excitement of pushing the envelope.	

You may find your students and yourself revisiting and refining the Learner Profile from time to time, as you gain additional insights into yourself as a learner. Strive to use this tool as a means of measuring your growth in understanding yourself. It isn't necessary to have it be perfectly, totally correct the first time. The development of the Personal Learning Profile also helps to emphasize that we are not just one Pattern but all four. This is essential to understanding the totality of an individual's Patterns. It is vital to acknowledge that all four Learning Patterns are always present and valued. See Bonnie's Learning Profile on pages 29–30.

The Importance of Teacher-Learner Completion of the LCI

At this point, we strongly urge you to go online to take the LCI and receive validated scores and an individual interpretation of them. You may do this at http://www.lcrinfo.com/take_lci.shtml. Then click on "Adult Education Form."

It is critical that teacher-learners complete the LCI and spend time comparing what their scores mean vis-a-vis their lesson plans, their classroom setup, and their manner of giving directions for learning tasks. Teacher-learners need to be prepared to share this information with their students.

Also with your LCI scores in hand, you will be able to examine and understand yourself as a learner while reading this book. Everything you have yet to read will make infinitely more sense if you take the LCI now—and infinitely less if you don't.

The Third Tool: The Word Wall

Scores on the LCI mark the beginning, not the end, of the LML Process. Once learners understand their LCI scores, they are ready to begin preparing themselves to use the totality of the Advanced Learning System to do task analysis. Once teacher-learners and student-learners have a good grasp of their personal team of Patterns, they can prepare to develop the next skills in the LML Process.

The third tool, the Word Wall, allows the Decoding of a learning task to understand it as the teacher intended. In other words, "What Learning Pattern(s) does the task require you to use to accomplish it effectively?" More specifically, "What Patterns in what ranges does the task ask you to use?"

A valuable LML tool to use when doing task analysis is the Word Wall shown in Figure 1.8. It consists of words organized under each Pattern designation that "cue" students to the primary Learning Pattern(s) required by the specific task. This tool facilitates rapid and relevant task analysis. Students of all ages find using the Word Wall a quick and effective aid.

To use the Word Wall, simply compare the written or spoken directions of a learning task against the cue words found on the Word Wall. Circle all words found within the assignment beginning with the verbs. Next, circle specific adverbs and adjectives that indicate the degree to which a specific Pattern is to be used. Now you are ready to Decode

Figure 1.8   Word Wall

Sequence Cue Words		Precise Cue Words	
alphabetize	order	accurately	explain
arrange	organize	calibrate	facts
classify	outline	certainty	identify
develop	plan	describe	label
distribute	put in order	detail	measure
group	sequence	document	observe
in a series	show a sample	exact	specific
list	show an array	examine	write
Technical Cue Words		**Confluent Cue Words**	
assemble	erect	brainstorm	improvise
combat engineer	experience	carefree	incredible
build	figure out	create	independence
concrete	graphically represent	different	invent
construct	just do it	dream-up	risk
demonstrate	visualize	far fetched	take a chance
draw (drafting)	problem-solve	ideas	unique
engineer	tools	imagine	unusual

the task. Decoding does not require a decoder ring; it requires knowledge of the Learning Patterns and an awareness of what types of Patterns are required to complete the task successfully. For example, if a teacher asks students to identify three causes of the American Revolution and explain each, the student can analyze this task by looking at its key verbs and nouns and identifying what Learning Pattern each calls for. In this case, the words "identify" and "explain" are the key words that will direct the student's response. These words call for the Pattern of Precision to be used extensively. For more detail on how to perform task analysis using the Word Wall, see the Appendix.

The Skill of Listening to the Internal Talk of Your Patterns: Metacognating

Metacognition in the LML lexicon is defined as our internal chatter or talk—the voices of our Patterns talking, arguing, negotiating how to proceed, how to achieve—how to reach our learning goals. The internal chatter of a learner's Patterns becomes most active after a learning task has been analyzed and the learner is confronted with the reality of what is expected. A broad description of internal or self-talk, including Pattern associated talk, appears in Figures A.1–A.8 in the Appendix. The LML Process helps learners tune in directly to this chatter within themselves and formulate strategies to use their Patterns with intention.

The skill learners apply when using their four Learning Patterns with intention is called the Metacognitive Drill. LML uses seven verbs to describe the Metacognitive Drill: (1) Mull, (2) Connect, (3) Rehearse, (4) Express, (5) Assess, (6) Reflect, and (7) Revisit. These phases are found in the Appendix under Metacognitive Drill. Definitions of the terms are also found in the Glossary.

Teachers who are aware of the power of metacognition and the "chatter" occurring in the learners within the classroom will often use this lexicon of metacognitive terms to check on how students are progressing. For example, how many are still Mulling 10 minutes into an assignment? How many have Connected and moved on to quiet Rehearsal? Who has skipped these processes and moved on to Express or even Assess? Knowing how various learners are responding to a given assignment and having the terms to explain progress or lack thereof in nonpejorative terms can enhance both the learning environment and the teacher's ability to respond and intervene appropriately.

The Fourth Tool That FITs the Learner to the Task

Once learners have Decoded a specific learning task and listened to the internal talk among their Patterns, they frequently find their Patterns and the task requirements are mismatched. If that is the case, they need to modify their personal Patterns to align them with what the task requires. Although learners cannot stretch or hold back their Patterns for long periods, they can, with practice, achieve a temporary and limited modification of the degree to which they use each Pattern. We refer to this as FITing the learner to the task using the tools of Forge, Intensify, or Tether.

The FIT Tools

The acronym FIT represents the three verbs Forge, Intensify, and Tether. What follows is an explanation of how each works to help the learner adjust to a specific task.

- **Forge** requires learners to increase the use of their Avoid level of a specific Learning Pattern to succeed in completing a specific task. An individual can Forge the use of a Pattern by as much as five points on the LCI scale for a limited time. Forging requires intention, strategies, and focused energy.

- **Intensify** requires learners to apply their Use As Needed Pattern(s) more forcefully. An individual can Intensify use of a Pattern by as much as five points for a limited time. Intensifying requires intention, strategies, and focused energy.

- **Tether** requires learners to restrain their use of a Use First Learning Pattern. This is done by pulling back and limiting the use of a Pattern that would otherwise mislead or dominate the learner's ability to redirect effort to meet the task at hand.

The Fifth Tool That Pulls It all Together: The Strategy Card

The Strategy Card is an immediate and powerfully useful tool. It summarizes into one instrument all of the previously mastered LML skills and tools: understanding Patterns, describing one's personal use of Patterns (the Learner Profile), dissecting the task (Decoding), listening to the chatter of one's Patterns (metacognating), and identifying what degree of response is required to achieve success on a specific assignment (FITing). The Strategy Card is illustrated in Figure 1.9. It is a powerful tool for staying on task and accomplishing a specific learning assignment.

Figure 1.9   Strategy Card

	Sequence	Precision	Technical Reasoning	Confluence
Your LCI Scores				
Your Description of Your Learning Patterns				
How do you naturally use each of your Learning Processes? (Look at your Personal Learning Profile for the descriptions asked for here.)				

	Sequence	Precision	Technical Reasoning	Confluence
Your Analysis of the Learning Patterns Needed to Complete the Task (See the Decoded Task Directions)				
What does the assigned task require each of your Learning Processes to do? (Look at the Decoded task and determine each Pattern being required.)				
Your Strategies for Using Your Learning Patterns Most Effectively				
How can you Forge, Intensify, or Tether your Learning Processes to complete the task successfully?				

To complete a Strategy Card simply follow the directions provided in the far-left gloss of the card. Use the data you have accumulated about your Learning Patterns (LCI Pattern scores and your Learning Profile) and your skills of Decoding (task analysis), listening to your Patterns (metacognition), and FITing to develop your Strategy Card with intention. See Bonnie's Strategy Card on pages 32–33.

The Overall Effects of Using LML Tools and Skills: Intentional Learning and Intentional Teaching

Intentional Learning is making the learning experience work for you by Decoding the task, matching the Pattern use required to your Patterns, and then strategizing how to FIT your personal Patterns to meet those of the task. Intentional Teaching occurs when teachers know how to use their Learning Processes with intention to shape the learning environment and activities of the classroom. Just like Intentional Learning, Intentional Teaching involves a conscious effort on the part of the teachers to respect, value, and mentor the personal Learning Processes of their students.

The Power of Let Me Learn's Integrated System

The power of LML lies in the tools, skills, and shared language it offers teacher-learners and student-learners to communicate about learning and learning support in real time. No longer is the learning of any child a "mystery" to a teacher or to the child; no longer must a teacher attempt to "read the mind" of a student or misperceive a student's response to a learning task. No longer must a teacher attempt to create differentiated forms of instruction to meet every learner's needs. Instead, all have a way to communicate about themselves as learners; all have a way of understanding, respecting, and building on the diversity of learners and learning tasks; all have accountability to make learning work, and when there are difficulties all have the tools, skills, and terminology to diagnose, communicate, and problem solve.

This is the power that the LML Advanced Learning System offers to all learners.

2

Meet Bonnie

Getting to Professional Change Through an Advanced Learning System

I came into teaching straight from graduate school, not recognizing the extent to which I was already acculturated to think, feel, and act in traditional ways, despite experiencing excellent models of progressive, child-centered programs in preservice preparation. It's taken my entire career and considerable self-reflection to process fully the tendencies I inherited.

It was my tacit assumption that the more prepared I was as a teacher, the better I would teach those in my charge. I felt prepared and was thrilled to find a teaching position soon after completing graduate school. I soon found my new students consuming all of my attention. Those young learners were more interesting than all the curricula, the lessons, and the various scope and sequences I had acquired. No previous preparation, however, proved helpful in my daily net casting—designing and enacting the many lessons I taught each day in the hope that as hard as I worked, the students learned as well. Teaching was a lot like fishing in those days: bait the hook, cast the line, and wait for the fish to bite.

I recognized that for some children my best lessons seemed their best lessons, too. They learned; they appeared engaged; they interacted with me, with classmates, and with the material. For other learners, my "best lessons" seemed to leave no footprint at all. Even my "next best" lessons to bridge those gaps failed to yield a good result. As hard as I worked, some students still weren't "getting it." It bothered me, for me and for them. What was the problem?

In an attempt to redirect my efforts more productively, I began conversations with more experienced teachers to shed some light on the learning mysteries I regularly came across. I must admit that I found most professional conversations about learning and learners unsatisfying. Seasoned colleagues had little substance to say about former students and how they learned. Dialogue quickly moved into suggestions-and-tips mode. The "Why don't you try this?" suggestion was frequently a by-product of our brainstorming and may have been a temporary help, but wasn't rooted in any deeper knowledge. I could brainstorm more lessons, too; it wasn't for a lack of another activity that I was struggling. I was looking for insight about the gaps I perceived between my teaching and my class's learning and the reasons to explain them. Some explanations proffered about why some learners weren't learning were benign; other assessments were disturbing.

The most difficult lesson I learned in my early years is that some learners are inextricably trapped by teacher judgments and rarely redeemed over time, either by their or other people's efforts. Some colleagues' biases were ironclad—once the adult perception formed a student's reputation, the die was cast. Once quantified as an "enigma," a "problem," the "disruptive one," that perception lived on. Teacher ability to speak about learner's needs was limited in scope and usually communicated in shorthand, broad strokes—"good student," "works hard," "does fine on tests," or conversely, "slow," "slacker," or "not working up to capacity." Packed with assumptions rarely challenged, it became clear that years of experience in the classroom didn't necessarily provide teachers with greater insight about the learning process itself.

Over time, I realized that we teachers consciously and unconsciously sort learners into piles: We honor some but not others. Over the years, I became more and more bothered by that observation. My concern increased as I recognized that teacher bias against certain "types" of learners doesn't end when the learner leaves the classroom. Too frequently, the learner carries the burden of having been labeled into adulthood. To me, that is so antilearner, so antilearning. The tacit message is clear: You are not as capable as others; you lack something needed to learn. You are not successful by our school standards: You don't fit here.

I eventually recognized that there were learners whom teachers just didn't understand. Further, I needed to figure out how to identify learners in a way that kept them from being a mystery to me. As years went by, I noticed regularly receiving the "mysterious" or "problematic" students in my class. Looking at my roster, I knew why some children were placed in my class. I found that for some, I could not unpack that mysterious aspect of their learning. So I endeavored to do no harm. But other than trying to be compassionate, I wasn't sure how to encourage these learners to build their capacity. I wanted to change this situation, change my professional actions within the classroom, as I noticed that each year my roster regularly included those students who needed something a little different. I needed a different, learner-oriented stance through which to understand all learners. I needed new and more effective understanding from which to advocate for students, to reframe and influence interaction in a more positive, less condemning direction, understanding that put all learners at the center. I needed to be able to see and name learning as it was showing up in my class each day.

The Catalyst for Seeing the Possibility of Change

I first became aware of the Let Me Learn Process, an Advanced Learning System, when I enrolled in a leadership preparation program at Hofstra University 10 years ago. LML was infused into the coursework and presented as a way to think of ourselves as learners first and as future administrators second. I was fascinated. It was the first time I understood how my learning and teaching are intertwined. LML gave me a new insight into the knotty problem that so upset me, the sorting of some students into a negatively perceived group, from which escape during the ensuing school years seemed impossible. Finally, I could relate the issue of negative teacher bias against some students to something concrete. Prior to this insight, I simply hadn't considered that the basis for labeling a learner lies in the contrast between how a teacher learns versus how the student learns. As I was challenged to describe the "ideal learner," the "one who drives me nuts," the "enigma" or most forthrightly, the "problematic learner," I was confronted by the recognition that students who appeared as "ideal" to me, learned as I did; those who were "problematic" an "enigma" or "drove me nuts" learned very differently than I.

Within the very first evening of being introduced to the Learning Connections Inventory (LCI) and my Learning Patterns, I concluded that the unfortunate group of students seen as difficult was those students who learn differently than their teachers and, therefore, don't learn easily from the way their teachers teach. With this realization, I wanted to learn more about LML.

My quest took me to visit classrooms where teacher and student implementation of this learning system is broad and deep. I saw children who mastered all the LML vocabulary, who used it interactively with one another and their teachers as a means of enhancing their learning. I saw children taking responsibility for their own learning, deconstructing learning tasks to understand what kinds of learning they required, and, with that understanding, designing unique personal strategies to address learning tasks they found difficult. I witnessed learners who possessed strong understanding of themselves as learners and understanding of how their classmates learned differently and similarly to themselves. I observed respect for differences in learning among other students. I saw knowledge about the learning of individuals directly applied to interpersonal communication, group work, conflict resolution, and test preparation.

What I saw amazed and inspired me. These were only third- and fourth-grade students! I saw the LML Advanced Learning System in action, saw how it was integrated into every element of classroom life and learning: curriculum, state standards, group interaction, students seeking help from classmates they knew could help them learn, classroom management, and homework. I heard teachers explain how they used LML in homework interactions and conferences with parents. My strongest impression was of witnessing authentic learning-centered, student-centered classrooms in action. And yes, there were teachers in these classrooms, teachers who also used the LML lexicon, referred to themselves as learners in ways their students comprehended and were formally in charge. They showed respect for individual learners and behaved in ways demonstrating the centrality of learners in their thoughts and actions. This LML, I concluded, could be an effective means for me to achieve the intentions I had for myself, striving for learner-centered self-change.

An Inquisitive Student of Learning: A Discerning Practical Professional

One benefit of having been introduced to the LML Process within an academic context is that I was also exposed to its research background and the literature that underpinned its theory. This too served as an important basis for my understanding of what makes the LML Process different from other explanations of learning. I became a more critical thinker when it came to discerning a "fad" from a significant advancement in developing my understanding of learning.

For example, early on, I wanted to know how LML was different from the explanation of "I'm an auditory learner" or "I'm a visual learner." I discovered that descriptions of how learning occurs have long languished as simplistic explanations for complex concepts. For example, more than a quarter century ago, learners were categorized as auditory, visual, or kinesthetic (Stahl, 2002). LML's theoretical basis builds on these earlier explanations of learning by updating them to match the current empirical evidence of how learning occurs. In the case of labeling a learner auditory, visual, or kinesthetic, LML explains that all learners are each of these because all learners use the same portals to receive stimuli to the brain: the five senses of (1) sight, (2) sound, (3) taste, (4) touch, and (5) smell. And only if a learner is sensory impaired (deaf, blind, or the like) is the learner limited to a combination of the remaining operative senses. Even so, the explanation of how stimuli enter the brain does not explain how learning works. It simply explains the first step.

Another dated and clearly underdeveloped explanation of learners I had been exposed to for years was the explanation of learners that categorizes them as right-brained or left-brained. Through reading and questioning, I learned that research on the brain using MRIs clearly indicates that activity within the brain occurs in various sectors as learning tasks occur (Dien et al., 2008). For example, when reading aloud, the brain is firing in no fewer than five regions. We now know that the brain operates as a whole rather than as a parsed or divided entity. In fact, researchers (McCrone, 2000) suggested that there are multiple sectors of the brain, meaning we can no longer accurately label a learner right-brained or left-brained. Just imagine, if we want to be truly accurate when referencing an individual at different points along a learning task. You would need to say, "Oh right now he's a frontal lower-external quadrant or a center middle-internal quadrant," and even then, that explanation would be only temporary as the learner moves on to another phase of the task.

LML's Advanced Learning System has built its explanation on the following current understandings of this relationship: LML embraces the importance of stimuli and their effect on the brain; recognizes the centrality of the brain as a megaprocessor of the stimuli, reasons that the interface between the brain-mind is where the processed stimuli are filtered through a series of cognitive, conative, and affectively woven mental operations, and concurs that the mind (our human consciousness) is where the stimuli are translated into symbols of language, numbers, and the like for storage in and retrieval from our different forms of memory (Bruer, 1994; C. Johnston, 2007).

Another area I explored was multiple intelligences (Gardner, 1983). After significant examination of this approach to understand learners,

I concluded that multiple intelligences can best be defined as the inheritance of talents that we receive as part of our genetic makeup. These talents remain hidden unless they are brought forward and developed over our lifetime. This aspect of our personhood is central to our human potential. It consists of the gifts that make us unique. What they are not is a framework for learning. They do not determine how our brain functions nor how our mind takes in stimuli and processes the world. They are, in fact, an enhancement to our generic humanness. We each have these "intelligences" or potentialities to differing degrees. They are not, however, a learning tool. They are a gift that enhances our humanity. Each is a kernel to be developed and nurtured.

LML often appears to teachers at first blush as another program or a twist on learning styles. It is not. Other approaches overlap with some LML elements, but none has its comprehensiveness nor explicitly provides learners with tools, skills, and a lexicon of terms whereby they can communicate their learning. Clearly, it was important for me to understand the basis for the theory behind learning styles. Ironically, I found when reading the literature of learning styles dating back to more than 25 years ago that learning styles have only a small theoretical link to learning. That is because learning styles are an offshoot of the Myers Briggs Personality Inventory (Myers Briggs, Mcaulley, Quenk, & Hammer, 1998). The Myers Briggs instrument, based on personality constructs as identified by Carl Jung, is a well-recognized instrument for identifying an individual's personality and temperament. Jungian constructs revolve around the affective domain emphasizing things such as temperament and social affiliation (introvert-extrovert). However, because it was not based on learning constructs, it is not a valid means for identifying how learning occurs within individuals. Its offshoots that sort learners by a shade of the rainbow (a color) or a personality type frequently fall under criticism because, as Curry (1990) and Heredia (1999) reported, instruments that measure learning style are popular, but research does not fully support either their use or the underlying theory behind them (Irvine & York, 1995). Evidence for the reliability and validity of learning style instruments is weak (Stahl, 2002).

Why the Let Me Learn Process?
A Conscious Choice

Choosing to implement the LML Process within my classroom was a conscious choice, and not one I made lightly. As a seeker of best practices, I have, over the years, completed staff development in and implemented into my classroom no fewer than eight major best practice initiatives including Understanding by Design, Differentiated Instruction, Balanced Literacy, whole language, CSMP mathematics, curriculum mapping, and cooperative learning. Just thinking about this makes me feel uptight—so many unused binders filled with my note taking—so many good ideas lying fallow because there was no framework to give the individual bones a body and a life. But when I reentered the graduate world of advanced studies, I became even more of a discerning teacher-professional. Therefore, I explored LML's potential for making a difference with a critical eye. I did so by asking the following key questions:

- Does the LML Process take into consideration all aspects of how the learner takes in stimuli and processes them?
- Does the LML conceptualization of learning capture learning in the real world and work with it, that is, bring the theory into the real world so it can be quantified, observed, and measured on a reliable and consistent basis?
- Will this approach help me understand myself and the students in my class in a way I haven't before, and if so, how?

With a degree of certainty that this was, in fact, an explanation of learning that I could embrace, I entered into the LML Process by completing the LCI. This was my first venture into understanding myself as a learner. I explored the explanation of the Patterns. Then I developed my Personal Learning Profile.

Bonnie's Learning Profile

As you read my Learning Profile, you will note first and foremost that I am a Strong-willed Learner (in LML terms, this is denoted in this manner: S25 P30 T10 C30; see Figure 2.1) I am my own team. My Sequence, Precision, and Confluence are at the Use First level. My strong-willed nature constantly has me feeling an internal tug-of-war among my Patterns as they pull me in one direction and then the next.

Another outgrowth of my strong-willedness is my need to take charge. I can swoop down on a situation, plan it, drive it, and attend to all the parts of it, even doing others' roles. I'll willingly do your share and mine in work projects if you would just get out of the way. That type of thinking gets me into the most trouble. This is what has kept me fixed on a lonely hill, with little prospect for growth. I regularly take on too much because I believe I can do any task well. My strong-willed Patterns sometimes have me ignore the difference between confidence and competence. I have to practice a level of detachment that seems very unnatural to me. Saying, "No, thank you, I can't" is not a well-rehearsed turn of phrase yet.

Completing my Learning Profile marked the beginning of my understanding of my learning and the strong-willed team they represent. (See Figure 2.1 for details.)

Figure 2.1 Bonnie's Personal Learning Profile

	Use First	Use As Needed	Avoid
Sequence	25		
Precision	30		
Technical Reasoning			10
Confluence	30		

Explanation

Sequence

I get energy from making lists. When I'm waiting in a restaurant, an airport, a lobby, before a meeting, or late at night, I generate them. I straighten areas, sorting, hanging up, rearranging, and cleaning. Symmetry is important. I buy things in pairs knowing I'll need two to have a symmetrical look.

Precision

I love words and everything about them. If I can't find a word I need to express myself, I'll make one up. I hate forsaking the aesthetics, the details, the small refinements that just make things look right. Unfortunately, there are so many small things that need attention. There's always one more important thing to attend that I cannot; as a result, I am often disappointed.

Technical Reasoning

Don't even bother me with fixing mechanical things that are broken. I haven't any interest (or talent) in making the dehumidifier work. If I can't get someone in to take care of it, I'm wheeling it to the curb and buying another one. It's one of the few areas in my life in which I have an appalling lack of curiosity.

Confluence

I see the bigger picture so clearly and often all at once. I have a hard time working with people who can't use their imaginations to "blue sky" and brainstorm with me. There are so many possibilities to explore. I have an idea . . . then another idea. As a child, my brother jokingly called them my "interplanetary thoughts" that are best left "on whatever planet that came from." I like being the first to try new things.

Working With LCI Results to Understand Myself as a Learner

Once I had a grasp of my Patterns, I could see the working of the various Patterns in my actions, hear the voices of the various Patterns in my internal self-talk, and feel the affective influence as various Patterns took the lead during learning tasks. My next step in development was to begin to use my knowledge to do task analysis. Put simply, I began to ask, "What does this task require of me as a learner? What Patterns at what levels of intensity does the task ask me to use?"

For example, writing this book. What does the task require? From Sequence, this task needs an overall plan, lots of organizing of information, paper, citations for quotes, and a sense of ordering the many pieces of a very large task. It requires a big dose of Precision's love of using words and desire to know much information, to process it carefully, and to complete the task correctly. From Technical Reasoning it wants persistence to solve problems along the way and detection of relevance for the audience—but from my 10 in Technical Reasoning, the task is not going to get much of this. From Confluence the task needs the ability to see the big picture amid the huge amount of information, to connect the dots among a million facts into a meaningful whole, to have many ideas about how parts of the task might be approached and pieces put together, and to take reasonable risks without fear of mistakes. The combined power and abilities of my three Patterns in the Use First range suit me well for completing this task effectively. Plus, I am a member of a team of three coauthors, one of whom has Use First Technical Reasoning at 29 and can fill in for some of my 10 as the team works together. I am aware of the fact that I will need to Tether my Use First Patterns when they get in the way of the team's progress.

Of course, my students will not confront learning tasks as long-term as writing a book. They are more likely to confront complex tasks such as the following: writing reports and essays, solving specific types of math and science problems, planning and executing a puppet show for younger students, making props for the show, playing a solo in a musical program, and taking state high-stakes tests. By developing my ability to do task analysis, I felt better equipped to coach my students in addressing the learning tasks that confront them on a daily basis. Early on, I recognized that being able to conduct learning task analysis has huge practical importance in school and out.

In preparation for my implementation year, I enrolled in a six-month accelerated LML professional development course. Working as members of a cohort, we focused on understanding ourselves as learners and on preparing to implement LML in our classes. In becoming acquainted with ourselves as learners, we utilized the lexicon and all major learning tools illustrated in Chapter 1. For the final session, our assignment was to make a public presentation to our colleagues describing our individual journeys of coming to know ourselves as learners through the LML Advanced Learning System.

For my final demonstration of what I had learned, I created a Strategy Card to keep me metacognitively aware while planning, preparing, and executing this learning task. I already knew that my greatest effort was going to be preventing my Precision and Confluence from conspiring to overcome my audience with an avalanche of words and ideas. These two voices would need serious Tethering to keep them from overwhelming my audience and me. The act of creating the Strategy Card shifted the lead to my Sequence, as I thoroughly planned for successful task completion. As seen in Figure 2.2, not only did I need to Tether my Confluence and Precision but also needed to Forge my Technical Reasoning. Look at the detail in the Strategy Card. Note that the second line shows my use of task analysis and the bottom line indicates the specific strategies unique to me performing this task. I proved to myself the importance and power of this learning tool by presenting my journey in a way that conformed to my intention and receiving positive response from my colleagues.

Figure 2.2 Bonnie's Strategy Card

	Sequence	Precision	Technical Reasoning	Confluence
Your LCI Scores	25	30	10	30
Your Description of Your Learning Patterns				
How do you naturally use each of your Learning Processes? (Look at your Personal Learning Profile for the descriptions asked for here.)	I like things to look organized, neat, and clean.	I like to share information. I write a lot. Words are my friends!	I can problem solve when I give myself time.	I love ideas! I'm enthusiastic about my ideas.

	Sequence	Precision	Technical Reasoning	Confluence
Your Analysis of the Learning Patterns Needed to Complete the Task (See the Decoded Task Directions)				
What does the assigned task require each of your Learning Processes to do? (Look at the Decoded task and determine each Pattern being required.)	Make a PowerPoint presentation of what you have learned.	I need to share information about how I have grown using LML.	I must use equipment effectively to present my story.	I connect the dots of my learning journey for the audience.
Your Strategies for Using Your Learning Patterns Most Effectively				
How can you Forge, Intensify, or Tether your Learning Processes to complete the task successfully?	Stick to one graphic idea to make things look integrated.	Tether! Limit the number of words on each slide. Stick to your slides. Don't add any more.	Forge! Use my equipment to maintain a comfort zone. Be familiar with equipment.	Tether! Pick one graphic that speaks to my idea strongly and then leave it. I don't have to share every new "Aha."

Bonnie's Advice to Teachers
Who Want to Implement LML

What follows are suggestions for launching the implementation of LML in your classroom. Clearly, my suggestions are based on my experience using LML, my experience teaching in the context in which I am situated, the grade and content area I teach, and my Learning Patterns. I was comfortable having the implementation unfold according to the learners' needs and did not feel I wanted either to follow or to write a didactic rulebook for LML. As I was (and remained for a period of time) the first and only teacher to use the LML Process with students in my school, each year I began anew, administering the LCI and starting with introductory LML awareness activities. Teachers in schools where this process is systemically implemented do not need to administer the LCI or do the introductory activities because they will be receiving students who have experience with these initial phases of the process.

Strict adherence to my exact protocols is neither necessary nor fruitful for you and your students; engaging in the spirit of the process is, however, vital. The activities of each month that follow in succeeding chapters show the increasing depth of LML implementation and our reliance on the experiences of the previous months. I incorporated these LML activities at various junctures to foster or capitalize on evolving awareness as students and I worked together. In the early months, I created implementation activities to stand alone. Later, I designed activities to integrate within the curricular units I normally taught. All can be adapted to suit the needs of individual learners in varying educational contexts.

Bonnie's Recommendations for Administering the LCI: Timing Is Everything

Avoid administering the LCI the first few days of school until students have settled into a comfortable school-wise routine and developed some rapport with you. Students need to feel that their reported responses are valuable and that there is no right response or high score to be achieved. Otherwise, they may attempt to strategize against themselves as they seek to meet their perceptions of your assumed expectations.

- Establish that the LCI is not a test! It is a learner's self-interview. Students expect that instruments administered during the first days of school are diagnostics for which there will be academic ramifications (pullout tutoring, placement in ability groups, and the like). They are not likely to disclose real data about themselves out of fear for how this information will be used.
- Familiarize the students with the LCI's response continuum so that students understand the contextual conditions for answering "never ever," "almost never," "sometimes," "almost always," or "always." The inability to discern among the five choices results in LCI Pattern scores that ultimately don't reflect the learner closely.
- Encourage students to clarify their responses when necessary, especially when their natural inclination is just to choose a middle road response, like "sometimes" when the learner feels no category is the "just right" fit. Those written responses give additional insight into the student's learning characteristics that portray a more accurate picture of their Learning Patterns.

Bonnie's Experience of Change (Bob's Perspective)

School is starting. For Bonnie it brings great anticipation; she begins a huge personal project, a year focused on how she learns and students learn, a year for changing herself and her teaching practice. She intends to implement LML with fidelity, to become keenly learning-centered amid a school culture focused on teaching subject content, not learning. In most chapters, this final section pays central attention to Bonnie rather than her students. It attends to the internal experience of a successful veteran teacher implementing LML.

In this first analysis, I want to focus on the effect of school culture. Throughout the book, the culture of the classroom is the analytical lens used to understand Bonnie's engagement in change. Culture experienced in classrooms has been amazingly stable for decades (Lortie, 1975). Its large function is to preserve social stability. But in providing stability, culture becomes a great change resistor. Further, culture's most powerful change resistant element is invisible, tacit assumptions, assumptions we cannot easily verbalize, yet they dwell deep within us at a subconscious level and guide our observable actions (Osterman & Kottkamp, 2004).

When Bonnie works to implement LML, she struggles against tacit cultural assumptions. She struggles with herself because existing culture is in her, and to change, she must work against herself to replace old assumptions with new ones. For example, "The teacher works always to be in charge and control," is a primary school culture assumption. But a primary assumption of LML is "The teacher works to have learners take responsibility and control for their own learning." The assumptions are clearly antithetical. As Bonnie works to change, she feels the tug-of-war of assumptions, internal tension, and struggle because real change always entails a degree of wrestling and awkwardness. You will see the previous example and others played out in this section in future chapters.

Bonnie and you will share this journey if you elect to implement the LML Process. There is tension. To hide this is dishonest. To include it runs the risk of turning you away. But for those who persist in the pursuit, transparency provides a touchstone to let you know you are not crazy; you are not lost. This is part of the journey.

Bonnie does make it—and well. "I learned more that year than in all prior years combined. It was the turning point in my professional practice. I became the teacher I aspired to be."

In reading further, ask yourself, *What is it about LML that supported Bonnie's change and success?*

3

September/October

Understanding the Self as Learner

Each September I am granted the gift of a fresh start, an anticipatable, academic do-over accompanied by new students, schedules, lessons, as well as aspirations for my teaching and my students' learning. It's a powerful image of possibility.

The reality is, however, that my attitudes, practices, and experiences from the past shape my present actions. There are truly no do-overs or clean slates for individuals or groups unless we bring new perspectives to our lived experiences and new strategies to enact the changes we desire. We all retain biases; identifying them is a challenge. My students, for example, had decided at some point in their collective past who among them was good, smart, and valuable and, by contrast, who was designated bad, less capable, therefore, not worthy of much attention.

The following two vignettes reveal situations I faced in helping students identify and confront those biases. These two individuals took the risk of making their private biases public, thus, beginning a new dialogue. These vignettes contain the first of many conversations with my students about confronting our old belief systems.

Vignette 1: "Where Are All the Good Kids?"

The kids are looking at the Learning Connections Inventory (LCI) chart I posted one morning. I administered the LCI, validated their responses, and generated a chart for each of my three language arts classes. Today, I'm sharing our results—theirs and mine—and beginning to explain the significance of the four Patterns—(1) Sequence, (2) Precision, (3) Technical Reasoning, and (4) Confluence—and the numbers associated with them. In truth, as soon as some kids took the LCI, they started peppering me with questions: What does Sequence mean? Why are there four Patterns? What makes it a Pattern? How do you pronounce "Con-flu-ence"? Why do we get numbers? Why do we have to graph our results? Why do we have to write our answers?

The class gets quiet as I begin to step them through how I organized the LCI charts. I see from their body movements that they are looking beyond me to examine the charts. They are clearly interested in understanding the symbols, analyzing what they see, trying to make sense of it all.

"C'mon, you can get closer," I motion to them, and they bolt up and crowd around the charts. There is a buzz as the kids comment to one another about the lists and numbers of classmates.

Jordan (S25 P24 T21 C15) is looking at the names and LCI scores on the list. Finally, Jordan speaks up.

"That isn't right," he says, pointing to the LCI chart of all the students' scores.

"What are you seeing there?" I ask him.

He hesitates. "Well, where is the list for all the good kids?"

"What do you mean?"

"You know, like for all the good students." Jordan lowers his voice in an attempt to rectify what he perceives to be an error on my part.

"If I'm on the same list as he is," he motions carefully over to another student (S23 P22 T28 C13) standing nearby, "then there's definitely something wrong, and I'm losing ground. We're not anything alike."

In this moment, I realize that adult judgments and assessments of their classmates have influenced the kids. They have divided the group at some point in their past: Clearly, there are piles of good and bad kids, and they know who they are. This is the first of many moments of disequilibrium during Let Me Learn (LML) implementation, as the kids and I confront assumptions they've previously held about who is considered smart, what constitutes a good student, whose learning was previously honored in school, and whose learning remained a mystery, or worse, was dismissed.

Vignette 2: Eleanor's Search for the One Right Answer

"Can I stay after school?" Eleanor (S29 P23 T22 C25) asks me for the second time today. "I have so many questions about the project, I could fill a book." I agree to our after school meeting.

I start the conversation. "I'm wondering what you're thinking about because you're a good writer and a very solid reader. I'm really impressed with your work." As I say this, Eleanor looks very small suddenly and unsure of herself, but she gets right to the point.

"Well . . . every project in this class looks different. I don't think that I'm following the directions if they are all okay." Eleanor points first to Hannah's project, a three-dimensional book that she constructed by hand. Eleanor turns to Dana's project, a colorful picture book sitting on the counter.

"So you were fine with your ideas until you started seeing what everyone else had, and then you started worrying, right?"

"Yeah. I know you said the projects could be different . . . but these are really different. . . . Look at this one." She points to a poster on the back wall. She's right. Austin's is completely different from the others.

"I just don't get how they all can be right."

"They're using their Patterns and figuring out what kind of a project makes sense for them to show what they know." I look over at the class LCI chart of scores to find her name.

"You're much higher in Sequence than I am—I'm a 25."

Eleanor checks the class LCI chart. "I'm a 29."

I laugh a little. "Eleanor, your Sequence is screaming, 'If things look different, then somebody's not following the directions, and I hope it's not me!'"

She laughs, but her chin is quivering.

"How do you know that the Sequence score is even right, that it's really me?" she gestures toward the LCI chart.

"Do you remember when you offered last Friday to organize the snacks for the book party? You were using your Sequence. You told me that if we didn't make a plan, we couldn't be sure to have enough food—or too much soda. Your Sequence is higher than mine, so it bothered you that we didn't have a plan yet."

She nods.

I open Hannah's "book," which is a box she's assembled to look like a book. Inside she's designed the tour-guide character and created handmade outfits for the character as well. It is very intricate, completely constructed from scratch. We admire it—it is very beautifully crafted and exemplary.

"Remember Hannah's race track last month? Remember she created the wheels for the cars out of those white loose-leaf paper reinforcements?"

"Oh yeah!" Eleanor and I nod, recalling the diorama her classmate made.

"She's using her Technical Reasoning and her Confluence. That's Hannah. Your project is going to be like you and reflect your Patterns."

"But I wanted to make a book, too; I just didn't want to make one."

"But think of your 'book' as a metaphor. Your book is actually sheets of paper. Hers is a box. Both can be good. Some kids really want to make something from scratch. Others want to try something totally different. You'll notice that even more so in the coming months. Things will be very different. Different is good."

I'm feeling bad for Eleanor. She doesn't like this message. It's hard on the ear of a kid who leads first with high Sequence. There's a look that good projects "must have" when the Sequence score gets as high as hers. I try to think about what I would need to hear if I were standing in front of my teacher, feeling empty. Even as an adult learner, when I feel that same bewildering emptiness, I also seek solace from an adviser who recognizes that my cognitive dissonance feels like a jagged edge in the moment I am experiencing it.

"Let's see your work so far."

She shows me her work in progress. I am amazed at Eleanor's thinking and her efforts already, as I review it with her. She's has color graphics, clip art, speech bubbles, and detailed quotations from the text. Her book runs several pages. It's thorough.

Eleanor and I stand for a moment.

"What do I need to do to help you?" I'm thinking about her affect. She seems a little relieved, now that we've gone over her ideas.

"I just need to sit here with you and work on this for a little while, I think."

"Okay, then. Let's do that."

Eleanor begins working on the computer adding text to her draft. I break the silence at some point and check in with her.

"How are you doing now?"

"Pretty good, I'm actually doing a little more writing than I thought."

"How do you feel now?"

Eleanor smiles. "Much better. I just needed some time to figure out what to do."

"And permission to be different, I think. Sameness is a lot easier in some ways, isn't it?"

We both smile at one another. She nods.

"Yeah."

Bonnie's Reflections

As school began, class members upheld inherited judgments about themselves as students: Some were "good," and others, by contrast, were "bad." I recognized immediately that the LML Process would liberate students whose learning was previously dismissed rather than honored. As nonpejorative LML learning language began to supplant the old language and ways of sorting learners into piles, the stir was immediate.

Including my Learning Patterns (S30 P25 T10 C30) among the class also caused a stir, signaling to my new students that some old ways of interacting would not be continuing in this classroom. From the moment I made my learning public, I began to see a powerful shift. No child was considered "broken" or a "slacker" in my room. In LML, I had the means to deconstruct those hurtful labels others had ascribed to my students and which some had internalized. I used LML to shape new, more appropriate learning identifiers for all of us.

What was also powerful, sometimes painful to recognize, was the extent to which some students had to confront their previously held assumptions about who was "smart," who was "worthy," and who was "successful." Jordan pointed out the *others* to me in class, so that I wouldn't associate them with him. Eleanor pointed out the others via their work products, wondering if she was still okay in relation to them.

> What was also powerful, sometimes painful to recognize, was the extent to which some students had to confront their previously held assumptions about who was "smart," who was "worthy," and who was "successful."

Both students indicated levels of unease with evidence of learner diversity because, at some point, they'd learned that school honors some learner characteristics over others. As a historically "successful learner" myself, I recognized the resulting confusion for what it was, and I was able to help students see the learning potential that existed within each of them and their classmates. There will be room for all of us here. If we honor some, we do not then diminish others. This recognition among the learners did not come all at once: We would continue this conversation all year long, each time the old attitudes resurfaced. The vignettes remain a powerful reminder to me for coming Septembers that my annual sense of hope and renewal, once only an ephemeral possibility, is now an achievable lived reality.

About Jordan and Eleanor

Jordan's insights about learning diversity were public remarks made as he observed learning differences displayed on the LCI charts and attempted to reconcile his lived experiences with new descriptors about learning. Eleanor's insights about differences among her classmates, in contrast, were private. I've been in their shoes, wondering, like Jordan, how my Learning Patterns were similar and different from those of my colleagues and what I thought that might imply about me or *them*. Like Eleanor, I've struggled even as an adult learner to reconcile my schooling and learning demands: conforming to teacher expectations about assignments, giving them "what they want," while trying to satisfy my needs as a learner, responding to assignments in ways that utilize my strongest Learning Patterns.

Jordan and Eleanor's concerns revealed the vulnerability they felt and their desire to figure out the different expectations in place in my room. Historically successful students, not surprisingly, are sensitive about changes in expectations. How else would they continue being successful unless they know the rules in play? Their admissions gave me hope that with greater trust, learners recognize that as their teacher my primary job is to build their capacity for learning. Only when they recognize my intentions as their advocate will they let me in to unpack their assumptions and allay their reservations and concerns. Only at that point, may I help them understand their uniqueness so that they can use this knowledge of self with greater intention.

What each learner expressed foreshadows what I will also feel myself later on in the year—the sense of vulnerability that change brings about in each of us, particularly when it occurs in a public setting. Transformation is messy emotional work. I usually like to control the outcomes and the degree of change enacted. Keeping tight control and making change, I realized, are anathema to one another. In these months, I am forcing myself to change my thinking about "good learning" and "best practice in teaching" in public ways, confronting the vulnerability in myself and helping students to manage it as well because I see now the extent of the learner diversity in this classroom, and I recognize that if I don't challenge myself to modify my teaching efforts, I will not reach these students' needs. Now I am seeing that there is much greater learning diversity in my classroom than I'd previously thought. It would be easy to dismiss the diversity I see as merely being a short-term challenge of *this year's class*. But in reality, I am seeing learners at an entirely different level than before.

Implementation Activities

Recall in the last chapter, I provided suggestions for administering the LCI to students. The activities below assume you administered the LCI and are ready to begin with the debriefing process.

Kids Need Initial Assurance That Their LCI Scores Reflect Their Self-Reported Data

- Reaffirm the total control learners exert in responding to the questions in the inventory. Self-reported data are the disclosures students make about themselves to get back an accurate picture.

It's all about them. The LCI is not the tool of a magician, a mind reader, or a judge. It takes a little while for students to recognize their central role in the process and to trust their efforts.

Practical Matters: Posting LCI Scores

- Post all students' names and four Pattern scores with some color-coding to indicate Leads (Use First), Avoids, or Use As Needed Patterns. The display should be in a visible section of the classroom, always accessible to all, and printed with large enough text so that it is easily read by the most distant student.
- Post your scores and consider posting those of other adults working directly with the students (aides, assistants, and the like). It reaffirms that the classroom is a learning zone and all are learners, not just the students.
- Keep the class LCI chart a conversational focal point within the classroom. Initially, it was the focus of specific conversations about Pattern scores and learning differences and was used to explain some LML lexicon terms: Leads, Avoids, Bridge Learner, and Strong-willed Learner. Later, it was used to validate individual responses to questions, activities, indicating to the learner how our Patterns are always in use so that learners began to see the connections among their scores and their thoughts, actions, and feelings in real time. "When you just asked me about the schedule for this afternoon, it was your 30 in Sequence wanting to break down the tasks we have to get done before we leave school today."
- Use the chart as the basis for forming effective teams for class projects (as discussed in Chapter 6).
- Post the Pattern attribute sheets as a visual reference to give learners a broader understanding of how their Patterns shape their thought processes, their modes of action, and their feelings about themselves.

Infuse LML Language Into Classroom Life

- Make a commitment to learn the LML lexicon terms and use them. Immerse yourself fully in LML language as an individual attempting to become fluent in another language. Intentionally infuse appropriate LML terms into all lessons, conversations, evaluations, and communications with students and parents. The rationale is simple: The sooner you and your students are immersed, the sooner all will communicate more effectively, more descriptively in ensuing interactions.

Other Places to Post Student LCI Scores

- Create a space on all paperwork you generate (assignment sheets, packets, pamphlets, rubrics) for the individual's LCI scores so that learner awareness is raised every time students begin an assignment. Include your own scores on your work as well, reaffirming your learner self-awareness.
- Label all final student projects, posters, and work products with the students' LCI scores, as a way of reminding the learners of their Patterns in use.
- Collect examples of projects that clearly indicate Pattern use as exhibits for discussion, helping learners identify how differentiation naturally occurs when we utilize our natural Patterns.
- Create individual LCI graphs for use on students' desks. The colored graphs (photocopied from the back of individual LCI paper forms) show the learner's LCI scores, and the degree to which each learner uses each of the four Patterns (Sequence, Precision, Technical Reasoning, and Confluence).

Display Word Wall Posters to Facilitate Language Development

- Post the four Word Wall (see Figure 1.8) posters indicating words associated with each of the four Patterns (Sequence, Precision, Technical Reasoning, and Confluence). The word list helps learners connect with use of Patterns in written directions, assignment expectations, conversation, and interaction with others and helps develop their LML fluency.

LML and Communication (Bob's Perspective)

The vignette about Jordan at the beginning of this chapter provides the first inkling of LML's potential shared by all of Bonnie's students. They are receiving their scores on the LCI, and they are drawn to this information about themselves, wanting to understand its meaning. There is "excitement and curiosity," and "investment," atypical in most classrooms. They "bolt" to see their data. There is a "buzz" of comment. They see their data and data on all members of the class, including their teacher. This is unusual; typically, individual information is not publicly shared, and it is even more unusual for kids to see personal teacher data.

It is clear that LML, by providing information about students as learners, created an atypical classroom situation. The resultant behaviors are ones teachers and supervisors seek: excitement, focused engagement, questioning, problem framing using data, the sense something important is going on in students' minds—no heads down on desks.

There is a second level here. Only Jordan and Bonnie participate in a "moment of disequilibrium." Jordan sees data that don't fit his assumptions about how school works. He has long been a "good kid, a good student"; he knows he is. But among the lists of kids with somewhat similar LCI scores, he doesn't see himself grouped with others he identifies as good students. The data don't add up for Jordan; Bonnie must have erred. Then an unusual student to teacher confidence occurs: Jordan tells Bonnie with a nod that *he* (a historically unsuccessful student) is also on the list with Jordan, "We're not anything alike." Jordan assumes Bonnie shares his assumptions. Jordan may not grasp fully what he has uncovered, but LML data have led him to a "moment of disequilibrium," a problematic situation with potential to trigger reflective practice. He has pulled the wraps off the deep yet Public Secret Number 1: that kids are categorized into groups as good or bad students for their whole school careers, groups that have privileging or devastating outcomes (Kottkamp & Silverberg, 2006). Bonnie gets this—the excitement of all the kids and Jordan's unearthing of a major assumption acculturated into both kids and teachers by school culture. Early on, Bonnie sees evidence that LML is changing and will further change how kids and she think and communicate.

Eleanor's vignette follows Jordan's. They are different but also connected. Eleanor, too, is a good kid, a historically successful student. Jordan's moment of disequilibrium was primarily cognitive. Eleanor experiences affective dissonance. She feels vulnerable, scared; she quivers at one point. She tells Bonnie what is confusing and upsetting: "Every project in this class looks different. I don't think that I'm following the directions if they are all okay. . . . I just don't get how they all can be right." She is pulling the wraps off another public secret.

Eleanor's success came through following Public Secret Number 2: There is but one correct answer; there is only one right way to do an assignment, a single model of goodness. As a good student, Eleanor knows the basic rule: Follow the directions impeccably and do exactly as you are told. But in this instance, that rule has not worked. She is confused, bewildered, and distraught. From the same directions, other students produced widely varied projects and got recognition from Bonnie equal to hers. How can that be? What is going on here? Bonnie changed the rule. Eleanor says in frustration and disbelief, "I know you [Bonnie] said the projects could be different . . . but these are really different!"

Bonnie demonstrates sensitivity to Eleanor's affective upset, and she provides Eleanor with a calm, rational, and descriptive LML-grounded explanation of the fact of much variation among students' Pattern sets and how projects vary based on what their LCI scores are. After all, we are our Learning Patterns. To demonstrate, Bonnie uses Eleanor's LCI score of 29 in Sequence—to which Eleanor, still in disbelief, raises a validity question. Bonnie compares Eleanor's strong Sequential learning lead with Hannah, who leads her learning with Technical Reasoning and Confluence and who produced a very different product. Bonnie points to several additional products, different from all others and concludes with, "You'll notice that [project differences] even more so in the coming months. Things will be different. Different is good." Though Eleanor seems more calm, the message, "different is good," is probably still unsettling. She doesn't grasp the full import of Bonnie's LML based appreciation of all learners at this point, just as Jordan didn't totally grasp the point about Bonnie's intention to attend to individual Learning Patterns rather than frozen reputations. What is probably inescapable to Eleanor, however, is Bonnie's caring for her as a person and a learner, a solid basis upon which to continue developing understanding with her teacher about her troubling issue.

What is clear in both vignettes is that introducing LML makes a difference for Bonnie and her students in feeling, thinking, and communicating with one another. Importantly, these differences result in opportunities for engaging in reflective practice and growth.

Bonnie's Experience of Change (Bob's Perspective)

Disrupting Marginalization

The public secret Jordan spoke openly is that there are good kids/students and bad kids/students. Everyone knows this: principals do; teachers do; kids do. These labels arise early and freeze; they exert tremendous power over kids' lives for ill or good (Silverberg, 2002). That good/bad categories completely overlook learning diversity is not recognized. In this section, we raise two questions. Where does this phenomenon come from? What is the effect on this phenomenon of embedding LML in the daily thoughts and actions of students and teachers?

Student marginalization is a result of a mismatch between teachers' and students' Patterns (Silverberg, 2002). Kottkamp and Silverberg (1999) found that students who blocked teachers from receiving their most desired reward, "the times I know I have 'reached' a student" (Lortie, 1975, p. 104), were categorized as problematic and marginalized through physical and psychological isolation. When teachers labeled students problematic, they were found to have Pattern conflicts with them (Kottkamp, 2002). Pattern conflict is unintentional negative interaction resulting from pronounced Pattern differences and lack of communication about differences in approaching learning. Problematic students do not learn the ways their teachers teach; consequently, they do not reward teachers by seeing them learn. The teacher response of marginalization—isolation—makes communication impossible and initiates a negative self-reinforcing cycle.

Osterman's (2000) literature review found a direct link between teacher treatment of students and peer acceptance or rejection of them: "Teacher preferences and patterns of interactions with students . . . influence . . . peer relationships, with peer acceptance mirroring teacher preferences" (p. 339). Thus, when teachers marginalize and isolate students in the public space of the classroom because of unrecognized Pattern conflict, their peers learn to categorize, marginalize, and isolate them as well. Silverberg (2002) argued that marginalized students receive inequitable treatment: negative outcomes rather than positive ones accruing from teacher acceptance and positive interaction. The opposite case can be made: Kids with the frozen status good are treated inequitably because they are privileged and receive more teacher acceptance and time resulting in positive academic and social outcomes. In broad strokes, the good/bad categories so upsetting to Bonnie result from students observing how teachers unintentionally treat students differentially.

How does LML address the marginalization cycle? The marginalization cycle is held in place by "prescriptive" thinking and language grounded in judgment. Jordan's nod toward the unnamed bad kid was prescriptive. Jordan was judging: *He* is lower than I am. But direct discussion of LCI scores opened Jordan's use of descriptive language, language depicting simply fact, what is: I am grouped with him based on our similar LCI scores. This is not judgment but data grounded, fact-focused language. To engage in reflective practice, we must break our custom of thinking primarily in prescriptive/judgmental language by shifting to data about our behaviors and use of descriptive/factual language (Osterman & Kottkamp, 2004). LML focuses us on data and descriptive language; it enables reflective thinking.

LML focuses us on how kids and adults alike learn. Doing so, it explicitly grants equal worth and importance to each of the four Patterns. There is no hierarchy. None is superior, none inferior. We possess—we are—all four Patterns, though their levels differ from person to person. LML focuses us on data-grounded analysis of ourselves and others as learners, on analysis of learning tasks we confront, on developing individual strategies to create intentional, better matches between tasks and our Patterns—or between teacher and student with very different Pattern teams. The LML lexicon enables us to externalize our learning in real time. LML requires us to use descriptive, fact-based thought and language in doing these things.

One great potential of LML is to liberate us from unknowingly freezing kids in good/bad categories for their entire school lives, from unintentionally privileging some while marginalizing others (Kottkamp & Silverberg, 2006). In focusing on each child as a learner and using the lexicon, we engage one another on a basis more relevant to school purpose than we have had available before. LML moves us from "every child can learn" thinking (a prescription resting on the unarticulated assumption "as long as he or she learns the way I do and school privileges") to descriptive "every child learns" thinking (resting on the explicit assumption that learning is already and always going on; we just need to appreciate diversity for what it is.)

> One great potential of LML is to liberate us from unknowingly freezing kids in good/bad categories for their entire school lives, from unintentionally privileging some while marginalizing others.

For those of us who teach, no rewards come from marginalizing students; we cannot reach those we push away. LML's potential is for us to garner greater teaching rewards because in becoming intentional teachers we facilitate every child's learning.

Seeing and Working With
the Elephant in the Classroom

Eleanor is concerned; she temporarily loses her sense of security from following the rules, which had provided success for her in the past. Bonnie assures her that she remains successful *and* that difference is good. If we step back and widen our perspective, we may begin to see the elephant in the room: the wide learner diversity present in most classrooms, certainly in Bonnie's.

Educators are familiar with research on various forms of diversity and its effects on schools and individual outcomes: parent socioeconomic status, ethnic subculture, first language, race, class, and gender. Teachers are aware of special needs categories. And though educators are acquainted with ideas of multiple intelligences and learning styles, these approaches have not proven to be practical in identifying how learning differences play themselves out in real-time classroom situations. Without such practical applications, the elephant remains largely invisible—undiscussable—and very much in the room.

Diversity in children's learning is both the largest and the most invisible source of diversity we interact with on a daily basis. LML is completely unlike programs that type students through some kind of instrument and then leave it to the teacher to teach to each different category—to differentiate by increasing the amount of teacher work. Rather, LML provides understanding and practical tools to allow teachers and kids alike to see and work with learning diversity, to be intentional about and in charge of their learning and teaching.

> Diversity in children's learning is both the largest and the most invisible source of diversity we interact with on a daily basis.

Does reading this chapter create any sense of unease within you about learners in the past or present you may not have understood?

4

November

Accepting Others as Learners

It was the ninth week of school, and we'd settled into an ordinary reading lesson in which we listened to classmates read their written reflections. By this time, students knew I expected participation from all in reading their work. I had become more deeply committed to 100% participation now than ever before because I was gaining an understanding of why some learners in the past participated readily while others seemed invisible or slunk into their seats.

Vignette 1: Responses to *The Giver*

The kids have written responses to how they think wisdom and suffering are related, derived from the major theme in The Giver, *a novel they are reading.*

"Why are those two things linked so frequently? What do we learn from suffering or tragedy that makes us wise?" I had asked the class the night before. This afternoon Kimberly reads first.

She reads a very poignant story about her grandmother dying and the routine she remembers of going over to her house every four days. She learns about taking every occasion, especially good-bye, as the opportunities they are. She talks about the power of memory and how ritual is important.

This is way more than I had expected her to share. The class is moved, visibly. Kimberly smiles at the end, but her eyes are glassy. The class does its silent clapping used for acknowledging serious writing. It seems inappropriate to clap loudly. I feel the emotion in the air—it's fragile.

"Wow, Kimberly. I'm feeling that you've taken your heart and just given it to us. I feel it sitting right here."

My eyes begin to smart. I could easily lose my composure here, but I want to redirect this, so I'm trying to manage what I'm feeling. I say to the class, "Wow." Heads nod. There's a moment of quiet.

Emma gets up. "I'm next. Yeah, I have a really sad one, but it's good, too." She scans the room. "Remember yesterday?"

Emma talks to the class as if we're all sitting around the dining table at home. She is really willing to throw herself out there without worrying what the other kids think.

Emma says, "I'm going to read to you about my grandfather, today." She begins reading, and at the end of her reflection, her voice breaks a little.

"I started writing this a while back, and then I added a new section. This is it. . . ."

This is what Emma came in to talk about after school a month ago, what she wanted to frame out with me, and did. I'm on the edge of my seat. Every pair of eyes is on her. The kids clap for Emma when she finishes. Some do the silent finger clapping.

I ask the class, "How are we doing?" I am waving my hands near my eyes. "There is such honesty in your writing. I am bowled over by your insights and maturity, I have to tell you."

Rachel stands up with her book and then sits down. "Can I have a minute? Can someone else go next? I want to add something first."

Matthew interrupts and tells about a grandmother who no longer remembered who she was and thought Matthew was her brother who had died years before. "She stopped remembering her age and thought she was 90 for a long time."

"That's hard," I say.

Matthew continues, "That's like Kimberly's in a way because the memory of the person is there, but they're not physically here."

"Wow, you guys. This is big."

Rachel reads about Corky, her dog. She made a PowerPoint presentation on Corky two weeks ago. Today is different. She writes about the day the vet came to the house to put Corky to sleep. Rachel's a very low-key kid on the surface. You would think she's calm because it's hard to read her, but she's intense below the surface.

I can hear sniffling. The students are moved by her story, and they find it difficult to look at Rachel as she talks. At the same time, they are listening to her. By the time Rachel describes holding her dog until she feels him getting cold, her voice breaks and stops. She puts her finger up in the air.

"I am going to finish," she says. At this point, I am watching the students watch her. The tenderness is very palpable. I've never had this before, but it is wonderful to see such caring for one another. I'm scanning the class. Should we continue? Do I need to say anything?

Rachel finishes her story about Corky and what her father said about dogs needing to be able to get up and greet you.

"When they can't, it's only fair to let them go, even though it's really hard."

This is the kid who felt this morning that she had nothing to say in her writing.

I ask the class, "Are we okay? Do we want to take a break?"

"No—keep going!" It's a resounding affirmation.

The class is experiencing something powerful, a degree of acceptance not before experienced within the classroom.

Mira reads next. "I now have two members of my family who have cancer," she begins, "and they've only given my grandma three more weeks to live. . . ." Her voice breaks.

As I attempt to process the enormity of loss that these children have been willing to share today, I continue to scan the room. They are all present in this moment, these children who clearly understand this thematic and very personal connection between wisdom and suffering. To their credit, they are not backing away from this new community experience—in fact, they are taking it head-on. I admire the bravery it requires to reveal such personal experiences—schools and classrooms traditionally don't honor the affective aspect of learning. I tell the class how proud I am of them for being so brave and taking care of one another.

I'm amazed by what we've just experienced: deep respect for one another, evidenced by empathetic listening, caring, and engagement. They are seeing one another differently, perhaps for the first time. In my years teaching, I've never experienced anything quite like this either. This moment of class community would be recalled all year long.

Bonnie's Reflections on Affect, Learning, and Community

The writing prompt that triggered the students' writing in this vignette, and other prompts that followed in the course of the year, had been designed to help students make connections among the narrative text, the themes of the book, and readers' life experiences. I specifically design this and other lessons to fulfill New York State English Language Arts Learning Standards, in this case Number 3:

> Students will read, write, listen, and speak for critical analysis and evaluation. As listeners and readers, students will analyze experiences, ideas, information, and issues presented by others using a variety of established criteria. As speakers and writers, they will present, in oral and written language and from a variety of perspectives, their opinions and judgments on experiences, ideas, information and issues. (New York State Education Department, 2009)

As a scaffold to help them prepare for the upcoming New York State Assessments, in which they will be required to draw information from a variety of reading sources and craft constructed responses, I require students each day to support various opinions with quoted material derived from the texts we are currently reading. This is a routine of daily reading and writing practiced in many classrooms.

As students, in turn, shared their unique perspectives this day, they noticed common threads among the theme of the books they were reading and to their own and their classmates' lives, which I believe emboldened them to take greater risks and continue to offer their perspectives. My introduction of Let Me Learn (LML)—especially the specific focus on each and every student as a learner—had modified the class environment in ways I had not experienced in previous years. The more intimate getting-to-know-you-as-learner experiences of this approach created a platform of evolving safety and trust on which the events of this special, unexpected day of sharing played out. I had not intentionally used LML to build the platform, but in retrospect, I see how my implementation supported student risk taking and honesty in their writing and speaking. It enhanced my established practices of creating a classroom in which safety from censure or ridicule is a primary safety net for taking risks and sharing divergent ideas.

As a teacher, I view myself as an instructional environment builder. And historically, I have viewed that as exclusively within my domain: I am in charge of the classroom environment—keeping it positive, healthy, and productive for the learners within. What I learned from the interaction was that the children not only understood it was a safe environment to share private thinking and take public risks but also that they were willing to uphold the conditions for that environment, through their caring actions and empathetic responses to one another.

This experience challenged my assumptions about student intentionality. As a writing teacher, I say that I want children to use language to become effective communicators. I want their writing to have *voice*. I needed that reminder myself because, in retrospect, I had underestimated the degree to which students would write from the heart and take the writing prompt to deeper levels. The classes' actions proved me wrong. The learners' writing had voice that day because in addition to the more usual craft-oriented concerns about tone, word choice, and syntax, the learners felt emboldened to reexamine their life experiences and committed words to deeply held feelings. Their complete immersion in the moment, their willingness to take public risks, and the degree to which we all listened in response deeply impressed me. I was given an unexpected glimpse of a class-room environment I thought was ideal, a vision for what could be with these learners, and I kept thinking I didn't want this intense experience of connectedness to be a one-time event. I was banking on the LML Process to keep such possibilities open.

Rather than interfering with or derailing planned activities, this lesson defined and became the benchmark for future classroom events during the year. It stopped the clock, in effect, on my plan for the afternoon's "curriculum delivery" and helped me recognize the powerful role affect plays in learning. The class remembered this lesson throughout the year and referred to it because it was powerfully emotional; it engaged their hearts (Affectation) as well as their minds (Cognition). I realized how helping students see connections among our thinking, actions, and especially our feelings facilitates developing a writer's voice as well.

That the kids and I extended ourselves to sustain this moment, spoke to our need for a space where we were valued and acknowledged as individuals. I remember alternatively feeling unsure and conflicted at different points in the lesson, pressed by time to hurry up to make sure that we didn't run over the allotted time for reading that day—kids had music lessons afterward, special education appointments, and I had another lesson plan to teach during the last period of the day. Our interactions reminded me of my mission as teacher to establish a safe learning environment and foster development of my students as *whole* human beings—not just as reading and language arts students.

There was another insight in this lesson for me. In the past, I was concerned about managing kids' expressions of strong feelings. I wasn't sure how to handle them, frankly, whether directed toward others or me. I felt the need to pacify the child in the moment, and frequently, I sent kids out of the room to "put themselves back together," thinking that private feelings expressed in public interfered with classroom interactivity and that children needed to remove themselves from public view until more composed.

I recognize now how impassive I believed I needed to be to remain in charge, how I equated composure with control. I believed deep feelings were unpredictable and threatened order. I avoided class discussion that might yield strong responses. It took considerable time to recognize how my controlling hindered our growth. The care and support the kids showed for one another during this lesson, as they shared content laced with deep emotion, and their engagement in a topic they realize they've all experienced, raised the question of whether I was trusting kids with their learning. I've come to see these control-maintaining measures—shutting down situations with potential for generating strong feelings and removing children to maintain class decorum—as wrongheaded, as inhibiting their learning. In retrospect, I see in the events of this day, how I was becoming a more intentional teacher.

> I avoided class discussion that might yield strong responses. It took considerable time to recognize how my controlling hindered our growth.

Implementation Activities

The examples below are based on a single recommendation: Begin to infuse LML into your existing curriculum. The LML Process is not a curricular overlay, a separate unit of study that will preempt lessons, units, or rival content area requirements. I began by using the materials I already possessed in the units of study I already taught. I recommend the following:

- Analyze and inventory existing curricular materials in use. Note what Learning Patterns are present or absent in your materials.
- Inventory and catalog titles and authors of favorite read alouds or novels students will read throughout the year that reveal specific Patterns in use. For example, Gary Paulsen (1998), award-winning children's author, reveals his Pattern use in his autobiography, *My Life in Dog Years*. He writes extensively of his problem solving (Technical Reasoning) and real-world experiences in the text.
- Help students see the learning connections already present in the curriculum and lessons you are teaching. Sixth graders in my class, for example, read Lois Lowry's (1993) Newbery award-winning novel, *The Giver*. In examining the characters, the conflict, the plot, students recognized that the characters lived without affect, a necessary component of learning. Their community favored order and adherence to strict rule following (Sequence and Precision) over individual problem solving and personal risk taking (Technical Reasoning and Confluence). The story connections to LML terms were a launch point for

discussion about issues related to conformity, individuality, balance, rules, safety, and self-efficacy.

- Use student-created work as a vehicle for discussion of Learning Pattern use and learning diversity evident in classroom life. Teachers usually keep models of prior student projects as examples to show students. Begin to diversify the examples of finished projects routinely shown to students to reveal the natural diversity that is not only evident in the classroom but also recognized by you as being acceptable. Students will need permission to use their Patterns with intention without fear that their work will be viewed as unacceptable. Label all displayed student projects with learner's Learning Connections Inventory (LCI) scores. Use all regularly scheduled presentation days, performances, public demonstrations, and book parties as a forum for learners to investigate and later discuss the learner diversity that exists.

- Encourage students to find evidences of characters' Learning Patterns evident in the books they've read independently in the past. Charlotte, the spider in E. B. White's (1958) book, *Charlotte's Web*, for example, uses her Technical Reasoning and her Precision in solving the main conflict of the novel.

- Direct students to document the LML connections they've observed in their reading logs or in journals. Students indicate what books were engaging and which were or were not a FIT (Forge, Intensify, or Tether), using LML terms. By analyzing their data, students understand how their reading interests are mediated by their Patterns as well as the author's Pattern-driven language, literary genre, and subject area. Noticing and acting on those learning connections helps students understand themselves as readers using new learning terms and builds confidence in their ability to make other reading selections that will be a FIT for them.

- Encourage students to report out evidence of learning occurring outside of schooling contexts and Patterns in use outside of school. Have students become detectives, finding evidence of family members, coaches, other relatives, and friends using their Patterns in their lives and describing those learner activities. Students post findings on a classroom Web site, classroom discussion blogs, or the like. "I saw my father using his Technical Reasoning and his Sequence when he organized his plumbing tools before fixing a leak in the basement." Online forums are especially helpful because students have access to a greater

number of learner responses and will see a wider variety of
real-world examples of Patterns in use by others.

- Acknowledge Affectation's powerful role in learning. Students
  need permission to be candid without fear of censure or
  ridicule. The learners are beginning to make powerful personal
  connections to their work and their lives at this point in the
  implementation. They need to be granted the sanctuary to talk
  about how their learning makes them feel, given the classroom
  context and school realities.

- Provide frequent opportunities to check in and ask the question, How are you feeling? I routinely begin a lesson by handing out sticky notes, and ask students to debrief. The sticky
  notes keep the responses short, so that it's not overwhelming.
  On one side, students report how they are feeling. On the other
  side, they let me know what they need from me. I read the
  responses to the class, and we discuss where we are as individuals and as a group, noting how differences in our
  Learning Patterns show themselves. Here were four learner
  responses that came in one day.

  1. "I'm feeling worried about our author study. I'm afraid I'm
     not going to get a good grade. . . . Usually my mom has to
     help me with my projects. You know what that means. . . ."

  2. "Please help me get more organized with my work!"

  3. "I'm stressed about the homework. I now go to bed at
     11'oclock at night."

  4. "I'm fine!"

- Use awareness of Affectation to develop writer's voice. For most
  language arts teachers, getting students to write with intention,
  especially with voice, is a top priority. Some of the challenge is
  developing and scaffolding new skills, providing access to and
  studying writers' craft, and having understanding that writing
  serves an important real-world purpose: to communicate.
  Developing writers need to see how to apply their natural
  Learning Patterns to their purpose, strategize the gaps, so their
  efforts meet the demands of the task. Student writers who become
  aware that their thoughts, beliefs, and opinions expressed in words
  have power are more likely to share their thoughts in words.

- Model writing samples for class study that show learners'
  Patterns in use. We write through our Patterns, and our writing

processes are unique to our Patterns. What I focus on as a writer; how I generate ideas; how I choose my words to describe my thinking and feeling; and the extent to which I describe my ideas, revise my work, and wish to present it are also functions of my unique Pattern scores. By providing variations in writing samples, we reinforce that writing styles are not simply a function of a writer's personality, the degree to which he or she followed a formula, or the stylistic conventions of a particular genre. I routinely photocopy overhead transparencies of learner-generated writing to use as a starting point. The writer leads the class through a discussion of his or her thinking process and feelings about the writing.

- Make note of how class participation occurs and is assessed in your class. Participation is mediated by a learner's Pattern combination and is only one indicator of learner engagement. However, I am more deeply committed to a practice of 100% participation now than ever before, as I understand better why some learners in the past participated readily while others seemed invisible or slunk into their seats. Several Pattern-related behaviors become evident with regard to class interaction:

  o High Confluence affords some the courage to take more risks.
  o High Sequence and Precision urges some learners to speak out to ascertain or assert that their answers are the "right" ones.
  o High Technical Reasoning increases the likelihood that the learner will keep insights private and not share them.
  o Diverse learner perspectives will not be available to the group unless they are shared publicly.

Therefore, exempting learners from sharing their perspectives adversely affects the group in the long-term. Participation from all learners is necessary.

LML and Affect (Bob's Perspective)

In this chapter's vignette, Bonnie's overall behaviors during the reading event signal she may be trusted through honesty, openness, and risking vulnerability in revealing her feelings, through benevolence and reliability in repeatedly testing students' states of willingness to proceed with the emotional content, and through competence as a teacher in supporting individuals and the group during the lesson.

In parallel, it is easy to see student behaviors supporting trust, caring, belonging, respect, and community building. Although Bonnie, no doubt, would have evidenced many of the same behaviors in prior years, implementing LML has probably enhanced the seven behaviors perceived as trust building (Tschannen-Moran & Hoy, 2000). And as students use LML more, they adopt more of the same behaviors Bonnie has modeled.

Freese's (1999) study demonstrated a relationship between student perceptions of teacher caring and student engagement in academic classrooms. Two of her criteria for perceiving caring teacher behaviors were recognition of the student as a unique individual and recognition of a student as a member of the student role. LML's classroom initiation through LCI score interpretation and Pattern understanding focuses tremendous emphasis on recognizing all others as unique individual learners, that is, unique individuals in the student role. Thus, LML's focus on the uniqueness of individual learners parallels Freese's very definition of caring and should induce a very strong sense of being cared for by both teacher and classmates. Examples of behaviors resulting in feeling cared for are ubiquitous in the vignettes and implementation strategies in Chapters 3 and 4 and together increase academic engagement. Thus, there is evidence in both chapters that Bonnie's growth as an intentional learner and teacher is a driving force in evoking student responses and behaviors that teachers value and desire.

Bonnie's Experience of Change (Bob's Perspective)

In the final paragraphs of her reflection, Bonnie signals an internal tug-of-war experience, as she works to change how she thinks, behaves, and feels on the road to her goal and commitment to implementing LML. In response to her writing prompt—developing wisdom through suffering—her students wrote about experiences that evoked deep feelings. The issue is that they are presenting these situations as support for the assigned theme but in public in her classroom. This triggers immediate discomfort in Bonnie. Her reflection gives voice to her "concern about managing expressions of strong feelings." This discomfort comes from tacit assumptions of school culture acculturated into her: Children are hurt by emotional displays. They threaten safety and order. I must squelch the threat. In allowing the students to continue presenting their essays, she is trespassing against these assumptions, so there is a strong internal pull to shut this down *now!*

An opposing voice pulls her to listen to the kids themselves rather than making unilateral decisions. The voice comes from her learner/change agent role, as an implementer of LML. It is grounded in new assumptions: Learners controlling their learning is the ultimate goal. Learners are capable of negotiating with the environment, supporting one another, and taking reasonable risks to fulfill their learning needs.

In Bonnie's reflection, we see a specific bout between acculturated traditional assumptions and learning-centered assumptions. Teachers implementing LML may expect to experience a similar tug-of-war or related tensions. If we listen very carefully, we might also hear the countervailing voices of different Learning Patterns. Sequence is a conserving Pattern; it wants order or to impose it if absent. It likes rules and procedures. Sequence might say, "Bonnie! Close this emotion down. It's dangerous. You need order! This can get out of control!" On the other shoulder, Confluence is a change oriented and entrepreneurial Pattern urging new ways and reasonable risk taking to initiate them (see Figure A.5). Confluence might say, "Bonnie! Stay with them; let them go. Let them control it themselves. Take the risk; there's great learning to be gained." Ensuing chapters will track this tension and show us how Bonnie works through it, as she becomes an increasingly intentional learner and intentional teacher.

Can you find existing opportunities with your specific current curriculum into which you could infuse LML language and concepts to increase learning without displacing content?

5

December

Sustaining the LML Classroom

Learning can be fun; we sometimes miss its inherent joy by taking it too seriously. In contrast to the earlier vignettes, the next, "Thomas's Nightclub Act," is whimsical. In his antics, however, Thomas unwittingly reveals his depth of immersion in the Let Me Learn (LML) Process.

Vignette: Thomas's Nightclub Act

We're in the middle of several things during language arts—students are simultaneously working on Robert Frost poetry projects, PowerPoint presentations, and calligraphy. Thomas (S26 P27 T32 C21) arrives in the midst of the activity, a little late to class. His group is working on their presentation. I am conferring with Katie and Marisol about their Frost collage. Thomas goes to the podium, which has been standing in the corner of the room since earlier in the week. He notices I still haven't asked our custodian to take it back to the audio-video closet.

"Hey, Ms. D., I'll take care of this for you because you're just a 10 in Technical, and I'm a 32!" He checks the power switch behind the bookcase, unplugs the podium from the wall, and winds up the electrical cord. He reorients the bookcase and moves the podium out of the way. He regards the microphone, pauses, and gets a mischievous look in his eye. He takes the microphone in hand, stands tall, and strikes a pose—he is now doing stand up. We are his audience.

"Let me tell you about my Technical side," he begins. He waits to see some reaction from any of us. Several students smile and look up at him. I had been conferring with Laurie (S28 P23 T22 C17), giving her ideas for her poetry project, but Thomas' performance attracts our attention, too, and we stop. We roll our eyes and grin, but stand, nonetheless, looking at him and waiting.

"Well, you see," he continues, *"it all started with a few hand tools when I was a little boy...."* Laurie and I start to snicker. Thomas is very animated and convincing.

He switches gears immediately, breaking the nightclub mood.

"Do I have to do calligraphy today? I'm Technical."

Martin (S26 P20 T34 C24) pipes up from his workspace. *"I'm Technical too Thomas, and I'm doing it. Look."* He holds up his paper and shows Thomas his practice sheet, on which he's been scribing his letters in black pen. *"We are all four Patterns, Ms. D. says."*

"Yeah," Thomas responds, speaking directly into the microphone, which is no longer turned on, as if Martin might hear him better. *"But I'm really Technical."* He changes his stance and directs a cheesy smile at me.

"And I forgot my calligraphy pen today," he continues to speak into the unplugged microphone. *"So... can I borrow one of yours, please? Please?"* He folds his hands in front of him, as if pleading. I think to myself, *"That was a pretty quick transition."* He is really being quite charming. I hand over my calligraphy marker, and he nods his head in thanks.

"Four Patterns, my friend. You are all four Patterns," I remind him.

Martin smiles at this overheard remark, without looking up, and continues working.

Bonnie's Reflection on Thomas's Nightclub Act

At this time of year, the kids were using LML language and identifying Patterns in use in their classroom activities. This was a transitional month in which class activities—research projects about Robert Frost's life as poet; poetry analysis in preparation for the January ELA tests; and introduction of calligraphy, a curricular tie to bridge language arts to social studies (Middle Ages)—permitted students to maintain a status quo in applying themselves with intention.

The kids seemed fine using LML at this point. They were operating in the classroom sanctuary we had cocreated. Staying at this level of LML immersion would likely be quite comfortable. I, on the other hand, was experiencing the uneasiness Eleanor had felt months earlier. Things felt and looked different to me in my classroom. I noticed that my usual planning mode, "What I'm going to teach next?" had decidedly changed, though I taught the same units I had prior to LML implementation. By December, I found every reflexive response to lessons, activities, responses, and assessment was mediated by my new awareness of how the students' Patterns and mine interacted in our work. I took special note of how the learners and I were adjusting, how infused LML was in my teaching and their learning. I found myself anticipating learner needs given the new data I had from them about their learning needs, and I sought to recalibrate the pacing of lessons and our interactions to incorporate our collective needs. My usual mode and reflex of "instructional delivery" had been interrupted, and I felt its influence.

For Eleanor earlier, the question was whether that difference was okay. For me now, the question was whether the difference I noticed in my work was sustainable. I was working outside of my normal routine. My awareness of great learner diversity in the classroom kept me from slipping back into traditional, comfortable teaching approaches. I was aware of wanting to meet student needs but overwhelmed some days, still thinking that differentiation was driven largely by my working harder to tailor-make assignments for every child. I was aware of liking the classroom engagement, the sense of purpose and industry, but I was also aware of its cost—I needed vigilance in my every action to keep this productive environment going. I didn't want to slip back into old habits of being teacher in charge, but my fatigue was evident.

I had been very careful to protect students with Learning Patterns traditionally undervalued in school, especially those high in Technical Reasoning and Confluence. I wanted to maintain a daily sense of academic sanctuary for them. Simultaneously, I realized that many who required sanctuary learned very differently than I, and I found it hard to keep their needs at the forefront. I often misinterpreted their learning behaviors because my Patterns are so different: I hovered over them when they needed autonomy; I drowned them in details, thinking more must be better. I felt out of my depth: recognizing student needs, attempting to reframe them differently than in previous years (not getting started right away, fidgeting, minimalist writing, not checking in with me, just wanting to get started, lack of words, off-topic conversation), but feeling constant need to Tether my inclination to "fix" them.

I wondered how deeply I would be able to infuse students with LML and how quickly they would understand and begin to apply it. I wrestled with the notion that implementation is about depth of immersion, not length of time spent or number of activities done. The perennial issue of coverage emerged, my accustomed thinking about scope and sequence. Maybe I would be able to teach them a lot:

maybe only a few things deeply. I didn't know—which tried my patience. I wanted to know precisely. It was clear that rushing them through a new experience wouldn't yield anything productive. I wrestled with this notion of immersion and how it shaped my thinking, actions, and feelings about my work. I moved into new territory mindful that I continued to analyze, test, and sometimes find my old practices wanting. More than anything, I worried about what I might uncover about myself.

Implementation Activities

Students' Self-Reflections: Fostering Megacognition

I routinely generate reflection sheets and assessment rubrics for students to evaluate their work products. To become autonomous learners, they need to Reflect on their learning regularly and systematically and to develop strategies and perspectives on their work to inform their future efforts. To foster reliance on themselves and less on me as teacher, I require students to evaluate their work before I look at it. I want their unabashed assessment of self: their perspectives on their learning, in the long run, matter more than my (short-term) assessment of it.

The Robert Frost Project

Figure 5.1 shows an example assessment sheet for an independent research project on Robert Frost. Students research information about the poet and use the knowledge they construct about him to interpret the poem, "The Road Not Taken" (see Figure 5.1). Some students choose to work individually, others in groups. This is a transition-to-group activity, and I am interested in their decision rationales. Based on their choices, I ask them to debrief about not only the project produced but also the interactional processes they chose. How did things go? Would they repeat their choices or change them?

With class novels, we routinely study characterization, as a vehicle for detailed text analysis. It enriches learners' perspectives on the works studied; it simultaneously prepares students for assessments requiring them to compare multiple documents for parallel ideas. It also requires students to infer meaning from data, draw conclusions based on evidence and from different contexts. I ask students to brainstorm and hypothesize based on their research

| Figure 5.1 | Reflections on "The Road Not Taken" |

Name: _____ LCI: _____ S: _____ P: _____ T: _____ C: _____

I. Think about the following questions. Respond fully so I know what you are thinking!

1. Tell me about your project. What materials did you use? What does it look like to someone who has never seen it? What are its special features? What are you trying to show in this project?

2. Tell me a little bit about your process in either choosing to work alone or in choosing your teammates. Include their LCI scores and give me your thinking about how their Patterns worked with yours.

3. Now that the project is finished, how did the choice to work alone or with others work out? What were the challenges that had to be dealt with? Would you make similar choices or different ones next time? Explain your thinking.

II. Confer with your teammates (if you have them). Evaluate your project:

4 = Excellent	3 = Good	2 = Fair	1 = Not yet

_____ Interprets how you understand the poem

_____ Includes a favorite stanza of the poem on/in project in some way

_____ Is completed on time

_____ Shows effort (cooperation with others—personal best)

III. What is your favorite quote from the poem? Write it here. Use quotation marks, of course!

_____

_____

IV. Based on your research on Robert Frost, what do you think Frost's LCI scores might have been?

• What kind of a learner was he?
• Use what you know based on what you remember from your reading, the facts you gathered, his life, interests, or his poetry.
• Give reasons for your thinking.
• Use LML language to describe and prove your points.

findings about Frost: What were his (likely) LCI scores? What kind of a learner was he? What evidences do you have for your reasoning? What elements are repeatedly evident in the various reading excerpts you've read? Over time, every person we studied in reading or language arts was under scrutiny as a learner. What were their Patterns? How can we know this?

Teaching Calligraphy: A Vehicle for Monitoring Self-Talk

This month, I began to teach calligraphy, not just as a series of minilessons about ancient writing styles but as a vehicle to help students become aware of their internal self-talk as they began a new, physical activity that required them to apply their Patterns. Calligraphy works as a device to examine a learner's self-talk because most students have little, if any, prior experience with it from which to draw. Therefore, they have no automatic responses to the task itself and must observe my demonstrations (mediated by my Learning Patterns) and begin to engage in the task themselves (mediated by their Learning Patterns). Students and I monitored their metacognitive responses to this new experience and connected those reactions to their Learning Profiles. I ask them to consider the following:

- Do they require multiple demonstrations or rehearsals of particular motions or letters to feel comfortable (Sequence wanting repetition), or do they just experiment on their own (Technical Reasoning and Confluence)?
- Do they find themselves getting anxious when asked to produce an exact copy of a letter stroke-by-stroke (Sequence and Precision's chatter heard at a higher volume than the other Patterns)?
- Do they want time to practice what they've already been taught, or do they want to go on to new lessons (the tug of Sequence and Precision versus the draw of Confluence)?
- Do they want my direct help (Sequence wanting a model) or time alone to figure things out for themselves (Technical Reasoning wanting time and space to tinker)?
- Do they think they know a better way to hold the pen or to form the letter strokes (Confluence wanting to do things uniquely)?
- Do they offer these insights to others? To me? When they begin to struggle, how do they respond? How good do they feel they must become to feel proficient?

These questions give learners real-time data about their internal Pattern-driven dialogue. They are directed to listen carefully while they engage in this new calligraphy activity so that they can attune themselves over time to how their thinking, their doing, and their feeling are intertwined. Ultimately, my goal is for each learner to transfer this lesson on internal Pattern chatter to other subject areas. My intention is for them to recognize their internal dialogue during routine activities they've been conditioned to ignore so that they can similarly monitor and direct intentional and appropriate responses in those subjects as well.

Our Reading Interests Are Related to Our Patterns—Really?

Students wondered if their reading interests and book selections were a function of their unique Patterns. We reviewed books they had read this year and previously, looking for thematic and learning connections.

A powerful language arts unit taught earlier in the year is a literary retrospective, "The Books of My Life." Students physically collect books that influenced them, engaged them, and taught them something important, books going back to the earliest remembrance of reading. Students conduct book talks, study main characters, consider life lessons learned, categorize books according to recurring themes, and write about connections made to their reading interests in terms of author styles, genres, and topics of interest. They write Reflections about themselves as readers, sharing their interests and why they like science fiction, biography, or fantasy. Finally, they create interpretive individual projects that situate the designated books of their lives within the context of a personal hobby.

In December, we Revisit the earlier projects, looking for evident Learning Patterns in their books' content and construction. They have enough LML experience at this point to think insightfully: Why are some books a better fit than others for us? Which authors write in ways reflected in Patterns? How could we systematically find books we like to read by matching authors and genres? Which books capture or challenge our imagination (Confluence)? Which books deal with life realities or solving real-life challenges (Technical Reasoning)? Which authors give such detailed accounts of events that it seems we were there, too, in the moment (Precision)?

Making connections between our learning and reading selves seems easy for teachers. But students need to Revisit past books with this new lens to reconsider their historic choices. Some students realize particular authors don't tie up the endings of their stories, more frustrating to some Sequential-lead readers than to others. Other students identify authors who are "too out there" (Confluent), so they can't relate to the plot or treatment of the text. Other students recognize their love of reading how-to manuals, catalogs, and nonfiction (some of which historically falls outside of prescribed school reading curriculum) is their Technical Reasoning engaged by practical, useful, real-world information. Although students and teachers likely spoke every year about a lifelong need to read, this year they gained awareness and insight into why they individually made particular choices.

The discussion broadened as I challenged students to consider why they said they loved or hated specific subjects. When they said they could do math or considered themselves bad at science, I asked them to reconsider what Patterns were in use, how they were taught, and how they learned. They owned their learning to the point where they could apply LML thinking to other subjects even though their other teachers were not engaged with it.

Although reading about Pattern learning through calligraphy, identifying lead Patterns in authors, and how book choices and Patterns are aligned, it might be easy to dismiss this as "fluff" and ask, "Where are the standards and test prep in all of this?" Consider that Decoding author and dominant book Patterns is the flip side of understanding what is required to score well on a writing test prompt. Students who use the Word Wall in conjunction with Pattern identification are learning how to analyze the very questions they must respond to from third-grade high-stakes tests to the new SAT writing section. Learning to identify Patterns in self and as manifested in the world broadly is both an academic skill cutting across subject areas and a life skill, preparing students to achieve academic standards among other things.

LML's Effect on Student Thinking (Bob's Perspective)

December's short vignette focuses on Thomas, but the action is integrated into the whole-class setting in a way not seen in other vignettes. Thomas indicates his knowledge of his and his teacher's Patterns in a one-sentence exchange, "Hey, Ms. D., I'll take care of this for you because you're just a 10 in Technical, and I'm a 32!"

Similarly, Martin's two sentences give much information: "I'm Technical too, Thomas, and I'm doing it (calligraphy). We are all four Patterns, Ms. D. says." First, Martin feels he has permission to engage Thomas during a class period and to correct his statement; second, he is aware of both Thomas's LCI scores and his own; third, he indicates greater understanding of LML than Thomas showed when he proclaimed he was but one Pattern. The banter between the two boys indicates that implementation is moving forward, that using LML concepts and its lexicon is part of everyday public, student-initiated classroom exchanges. That the exchange is public provides all students the opportunity to check their understanding of the LML Processes. Finally, variation in the sophistication of LML interpretation between the two students shows that not all kids are together at the same place in LML development and fluency.

Bonnie's Experience of Change (Bob's Perspective)

Bonnie's internal tugs-of-war between stability and change are still present, not resolved once and for all. Her focal tension is sustainability. Will she be able to sustain the implementation/change level, or will she slip back into habit and autopilot where old acculturation reasserts itself and the continuity of the past—not the new—is sustained?

Some years ago, Christine Johnston, LML originator, worked with a total school implementation—principal, teachers, paraprofessionals, and kids—in a small elementary setting. The situation was ideal because all in-school human influences were engaged in implementation. What Chris noticed, and later corroborated in other implementation sites, was that the order of "getting" LML was kids first, paraprofessionals second, teachers third. (Note Bonnie implicitly affirmed this finding when she said, "I . . . was experiencing the uneasiness Eleanor had felt months earlier.") What Chris uncovered was not unprofessional teacher behavior, slacking, or sabotage, but a deeper acculturation into traditional schooling assumptions. In this case, Bonnie had 41 total years of teaching, undergraduate and graduate preparation, and public school student experience to uproot and replace. The kids on the other end of the acculturation spectrum had six years of formal schooling.

Note another culture-based tension comes into Bonnie's awareness as she struggles with sustainability. Garnering the reward of engagement with kids (Lortie, 1975) comes at a cost. Bonnie experiences fatigue because she is playing out the old heroic teacher role assumption: Be in total command and take responsibility for doing everything for every student.

Tensions also surface awareness. Bonnie's desire to provide sanctuary for kids who possess Pattern conflicts with the general schooling bias toward Sequence/Precision, her historic student success, and her Strong-willed Learner experience results in *her* intense awareness of a new world: how different the learning of historically unsuccessful learners is; how different their approach to the world, to school, to everything is! She develops excruciating awareness of her misrepresentation of them and their experiential worlds and, specifically, the customary teacher behaviors she needs to Tether through increased intentionality and metacognitive awareness. All the while, she is aware that she can't fix a learner nor fix an environment so that it is totally safe for kids. Kids will always live in a number of nonLML contexts. In this chapter, Bonnie's reflection provides bountiful evidence that she is becoming an increasingly intentional learner and teacher.

> How different the learning of historically unsuccessful learners is; how different their approach to the world, to school, to everything is!

Many of the learning styles products assume teachers can be universal fixers if they take full responsibility for differentiating instruction in as many ways as students need. As just seen, this assumption results in tremendous teacher work and fatigue. By contrast, LML provides tools for self-knowledge as a learner, task analysis, and Strategy Cards (metacognitive crib sheets) to support Intentional Learning and metacognitive growth for particular learning task applications. Many teachers fail to see the difference between LML's assumption that we should turn learning over to the student where it belongs, as opposed to the differentiation through learning styles or teacher-matching-learning-styles assumption that there is more work for the teacher to do *to* the students.

It is December; as LML implementation increases in depth, a larger number of tensions surface, not the least of which is the impending state tests—all a part of the culture and the reality of the classroom. The pullback toward autopilot acculturation is strong and persistent, and Bonnie feels an acute pang of tension about the extent to which she can immerse her students in the LML approach.

What does LML bring to the classroom that is different from all the other teaching orientations you have tried or been forced to use?

6

January

Becoming Intentional: The Turning Point

For weeks, the students and I had been in a happy, interactive stage, a "stay and play" level with Let Me Learn (LML). We mused about our differences and made cool connections to our learning history. Using a biking metaphor, we were on a leisurely, interesting path. Suddenly, the incline increased dramatically, requiring radical gear shifting. Some fell off their bikes, experiencing a wonderful aha! Others saw the incline ahead, looked over their bikes, and wanted better equipment. I asked them to use what they knew about themselves to make decisions and take responsibility for the ramifications. The stay and play stage came to a squealing halt as learners tuned in differently to what I was doing with them.

Vignette: Dina and the Tough Question

One day in early January, we were talking about the power of making resolutions. I showed my classes the Strategy Card I'd shown my homeroom the day before. Two girls, I noticed, exchanged a look. Dina (S19 P17 T25 C22) finally spoke aloud. "I don't mean to be rude, Ms. D., but what is the point of our doing this?"

> "I don't mean to be rude, Ms. D., but what is the point of our doing this?"

I loved her question and told her so. "This is the best question! First of all your Technical Reasoning is speaking so loudly. Did you hear it? 'What is the point of all of this? If we're really going to start using this and relying on it, should I? Can I? Does it have any real value? If so, why isn't everyone using this? Who will help us with this in the future?'"

I explained we were the first ones here, but there are many schools using LML extensively, including a neighboring town.

"Then why isn't anyone else using LML here?"

I don't know if they understood that "implementation" implied "firstness." In addition to being first, you are necessarily alone for a while. Is that endurable?

Then the floodgates really opened. Questions streamed out from the kids. I couldn't identify who was asking; it was a collective outpouring.

"I mean, how long have people been using LML? Is it very old?"

"Is it just used in schools?"

*"I mean, this has been fun and all, knowing how we learn. . . . It's been nice, but if I'm really going to have to use this, then I need to know a **lot** more."*

I got this—the turning point in the implementation. Now the real learning began. It was clear they wanted my assurance not as their teacher but as an implementer. They wanted to be sure that I had a specific plan for them down the road we were traveling—that I knew what I was doing. What were my plans for them? What would happen if they bought into this? This was the point where we moved to the next level of immersion because the learners were sitting on the fence momentarily. Many eyes scanned for my reaction. Was I challenged by their pointed questions? Did I have satisfactory answers? In this moment, I recognized that intentionality is not about having knowledge; it is about fidelity, making a commitment, and having courage. The kids were trying to decide whether to embrace or reject this.

Bonnie's Reflection on Dina's Tough Question

I was not surprised the legitimacy question came from a Use First Technical Reasoning learner. She wondered what value this LML Process had, how she would be able to use this information in her future, not just in her school life. I loved her quizzical look as she awaited my response. I knew by the change in class body language the other students were asking these questions, too, and listening for my answer. Would I take it as a challenge? Did I get it, or like many other adults, would I sidestep this for my lesson priorities? Would I have a satisfying answer?

Their concerns did not derail me. I had abundant confidence. I wouldn't process my reservations until later, in March—and in retrospect, I appreciated that my learners were questioning LML's validity sooner than I was. I was still in the enthusiastic stage of planning, engaging in the process, and watching the results. I wasn't thinking about the future in January to the degree the students were. I was focusing on becoming reengaged after the holiday break, making resolutions for the next marking period, and preparing classes for the upcoming state English Language Arts test (ELA). I had already bought into LML and been using it with intention in both my professional and personal life for some time. I answered the validity question for myself years ago.

Students wanted assurance their Learning Pattern scores were accurate. They hadn't questioned their scores or their derivation before. But once Dina revealed her misgiving and it was received with openness, it was obviously safe for others to talk about this, too. I hadn't thought their misgivings were taboo; there seemed to be no off-limits topic in my classroom, but it was evident they had been wondering whether their Patterns were really them—what did they mean? As one student said, "I'm more than just a bunch of numbers." My response was "Yes—we all are. We are endless potential, but this helps us to see where we need to point ourselves."

> They had been wondering whether their Patterns were really them—what did they mean? As one student said, "I'm more than just a bunch of numbers."

I am always concerned when question answering on surveys involves interpretation, because sometimes I just don't know *exactly* what I feel or think. I recognize now it's my Precision wanting unrealistic exactitude, yet it makes me feel I'm on shaky ground if I have wiggle room. Some kids forgot their scores were based on their responses. . . . There was no magic shell game, no figure manipulation. They were welcome to look at all their answers if they wanted to and change them if they reconsidered them. That made some nervous. No scores seemed ideal, not even higher ones. Avoids felt like deficits, except that I, their teacher, have an Avoid score, the lowest posted score for Technical Reasoning. I'm cool with that. Should they be worried, then, about their scores?

Some students were waiting for me to unleash a big secret: Certain Pattern combinations are better. When I didn't, they made assumptions: I was too nice to say it; I was hiding something. The scores defied logic: Who would want a low number when you could have a high one? When I talked about the ways in which being a Strong-willed Learner is frequently disadvantageous and Tethering is hard to do, they sometimes looked at me strangely. Isn't it about the "better" scores, even if it's hard to be you? And when no "good" list, no hidden hierarchy ever appeared, they were stumped. What is this really about then? The LCI was another school thing, and teachers had always forced them to do stuff they didn't want to do, so they'll just do it to keep teachers off their backs. It's not really relevant.

I'm grateful for Dina's willingness to speak truth and wonder aloud, putting voice to her reservations. I deeply respect her courage; her remarks changed how we interacted in the classroom.

Implementation Activities

With the January turning point, students realized I was asking them to move from passive understandings of their learning (stay and play) to active levels of engagement by assuming responsibility and becoming intentional. To take this important step, they needed to understand how to Forge, Intensify, or Tether their Patterns to FIT the task. To achieve this systematically, students needed to learn to create Strategy Cards. I began with a class demonstration of a learner's inner dialogue to show the natural interactions among the four Learning Patterns so they understood the imperative for making an intentional action strategy (see Figure 1.9).

Thinking of Pattern Strength as Volume Levels

I made the analogy of each Learning Connections Inventory (LCI) Pattern score to a radio, TV, or conversation volume level. A Use First score (25–35) is high volume: The learner "hears" the directives of that Pattern loudly, above the others. A Use As Needed score (18–24) is medium volume: The learner comfortably hears the directives of that Pattern along with others at the same level, like multiple simultaneous conversations at a party. An Avoid score (7–17) is low volume: The learner doesn't hear the directives of that Pattern easily. It's like background noise that only becomes apparent when other noises are tuned out, or turned down, like TV news droning on in a distant room. You know it's there, but it is covered up by louder foreground noises.

Task Analysis: Deciding When to Forge, Intensify, or Tether to Achieve FIT

Knowing how to respond appropriately to a learning task requires examination of the task itself (e.g., what Patterns are required for creating an informative class presentation, or figuring out how to answer on a standardized test) and intentionally matching the learner's individual personal tools to that task. Engaging in task analysis to achieve FIT requires an understanding of how learners naturally apply their Sequence, Precision, Technical Reasoning, and Confluence in the Use First, Use as Needed, or Avoid ranges and intentionally modifying that natural use temporarily, by Forging (increasing a great deal), Intensifying (increasing a little), or Tethering (decreasing a great deal).

Demonstrating Internal Talk: Meet John

Learners have four Patterns, each simultaneously emitting a different volume level whether high, medium, or low. Using your Patterns with intention means knowing how to pay active attention to, or ignore, the demands of each Pattern to achieve a goal.

For the simulation, I preselect a learner to demonstrate how his or her Patterns feel when called upon to engage in a learning task. Modeling internal talk is revealing, giving others insight into what it is like to walk in another learner's shoes.

John's Patterns are S28 P15 T25 C23. His Sequence (28) Use First loud volume along with his other Use First Pattern (Technical Reasoning) leads John's attempt to make sense of any situation. His internal talk of Sequence breaks down tasks into steps and says, "I need things to be organized, dependable, and consistent." With greater awareness, John may recognize that he can develop his own directions when those provided are insufficient or unclear. He can learn to use strategies to Tether this Pattern when he hears his internal voice saying in some situations, "I need more time to check my work." "Could I see an example of this?"

Much is happening within John's mind. He has four Learning Patterns in action simultaneously (Sequence and Technical Reasoning at Use First levels along with two others weighing in as Use as Needed and Avoid). As a result John will reflexively turn to his Use First Patterns in every situation—unless he becomes aware that they are not the best Patterns for the job. At some point, he will need to turn down the volume of his Use First Patterns to respond appropriately to a task for which their loud volumes are not a good fit.

John's Precision (15) is Avoid, quite a low volume. In its natural state, his Precision is not willing to research ideas or ask questions even to figure out answers he needs. It rarely challenges statements that don't seem right. Most likely whatever the task, John will need to Forge his Precision (turn up the volume a lot) to respond to the task completely.

John's Technical Reasoning (25) is Use First. While the other Patterns grab his attention because of their contrasting volumes, this Pattern causes him to constantly stand back and ask himself, "What is the purpose of all this? Why do I need to know this?" when attempting to understand a problem. He is aware of this Pattern's need for hands-on action to repair what's not working or to tinker mentally to get a handle on the situation and work things out. John's Technical Reasoning's volume forms one of his louder, insistent voices demanding his attention. Depending on the task, John may need to Tether (turn down the volume) of his Technical Reasoning to respond appropriately.

John's use of Confluence (23) is Use As Needed, a medium volume. He can read between the lines to get the big picture and enjoys brainstorming but he only takes planned risks when necessary, and on occasion, he Intensifies his Confluence (turns up the volume a little) to go out on a limb for an idea he believes worthwhile. If the task requires him to do so, he might say, "I know the way I usually handle this situation works pretty well, but I have a different idea I think could work better."

The four Patterns at their respective volumes are all "talking" simultaneously to John as he is completing tasks all day, every day. His unique Pattern combination affects the way he thinks, works, and feels; it shapes the way he values certain approaches over others, how he views the world around him. Thus, as John becomes actively aware of his internal dialogue, his Patterns chatting in combination, and recognizes Pattern attributes as they manifest themselves, he may begin to direct his efforts more consciously and effectively toward FITing as a task requires.

Simulating John's Internal Talk During Testing

Once the class understands how each Pattern communicates to John, I ask four volunteers to demonstrate the volume level for the assigned Pattern. They stand before John facing him and read directly from a Pattern characteristics sheet or read premade statements (I've designed) tailored to a particular task, in this case a state language arts test (ELA).

I announce John's task, taking the ELA test. He opens the test booklet and prepares to work in the section requiring him to read a passage and write a short response. Each volunteer picks the appropriate volume level representing each Pattern score.

Volunteer 1 (28 Sequence, Use First) keeps calling out Sequential directions, suggestions, and feelings:

I need to get going! What's the question I need to answer? I need to recall an example of this task. I'll make a list of stuff to include. I'll plan my ideas on this planning page. How much time do I have? Is this question like any we practiced? How did I do it last time? I made a chart. What are the directions again? I'll reword the question first on my answer.

Volunteer 1 repeats the same ideas until directed to stop, remaining the loudest speaker of the four.

Volunteer 2 (15 Precision, Avoid), at the same time, speaks in a whispering voice, reading Precision thoughts aloud:

There's a lot of information here. Too much! Words. Words. Words. I don't get it! They want me to explain what this word means. Who cares? I'm supposed to select a definition from the words in this box . . . What are they doing in the box? And why do I need to look for a word that means almost the same as the word, interesting? Why isn't the word, interesting, okay? Who cares about finding a different word? How many more words do I have to go? Will this never end?

Volunteer 2 keeps repeating Precision thoughts, relating them to the project, making sure that his or her voice stays in the whispering range.

Volunteer 3 (25 Technical Reasoning, Use First) speaks very loudly at nearly the same volume as Sequence:

The passage is two pages long! Do I need to read all this to answer the question? Maybe I don't. I don't want to do any more than I have to. I wish I could take a break and walk around; I could get my mind clear. These words are messing with my mind. Is there a way to make this work better for me? Why did they give me all this space for my answer? The answer's pretty simple when you get to the point. So why can't I just get to the point and forget having to fill this space with words?

Volunteer 3 repeats his or her list, maintaining a loud volume.

Volunteer 4 (23 Confluence, Use As Needed) speaks in a conversational tone louder than Volunteer 2 and softer than Volunteers 1 and 3:

The directions say to make my writing interesting. I have an idea but I wonder if I should try it? I'd like to use some of my own ideas, but I wonder if that's what the directions really mean when they say, "Imagine a time when. . . ." Should I take the chance and use my ideas or should I stick to the directions and use the models we practiced in class? I want to take the risk, but maybe this isn't the best time to do that.

Volunteer 4 maintains a consistent voice, louder than Volunteer 2, but not as loud as Volunteers 1 and 3.

This is a fun, necessarily noisy activity accompanied by lots of laughter. As the volunteers try to keep to their Pattern scripts at a consistent volume, and keep composure, the class responds to the racket. I serve as moderator, assuring that volunteers sustain roles for a short period. Hearing a learner's *inner dialogue*, even for a minute, is a long time! It points out that learning takes energy and is all encompassing. If we don't figure out which voices give the most appropriate advice to accomplish the task, then we function on individualized autopilot, allowing our natural Pattern volumes to dictate an inappropriate, less successful response to the question. Without intentionality, it's all chattering, tiresome noise.

John the learner is trying to take the test—thinking, doing, and feeling. His classmates create a model of his private thinking or self-talk, whose complexity we ordinarily would never examine and discuss as a class. I ask John how it feels to hear his internal talk made external. Is it an accurate portrayal? What are the challenges he experiences?

If the balance doesn't feel accurate as presented, I enlist John's help to recalibrate the volunteer volume levels to what seems more like him. Next, I have the class do a task analysis: What Patterns need to be used and at what volumes? Future assignments always begin this way with the class and me discussing what the task entails and what Pattern FIT is necessary for optimal learning.

Helping John Adjust His Patterns: Applying Strategy

The class and John decide how to adjust his Learning Patterns to the demands of the ELA. Which Patterns are well suited to this test? Which Patterns might give John unhelpful information? Which Patterns need to be FITed? After discussion, John physically turns up or turns down an imaginary volume control. The volunteers resume their talking to John as he adjusts their volume levels, demonstrating his strategy for intentional Pattern use. The volunteers respond to John's directions.

Developing Strategy Cards

Strategy Cards are intentions set in words to keep learners mindful of task demands, so they work optimally. For each important task, learners create a written reminder of how they use their Patterns, what Patterns are required to achieve the given task, and specific strategies FIT their Pattern use to achieve the goal. Strategy Cards can be written on index cards, for example, easy to display as they are working—or put on sheets of paper (I have students work on the computer; it's easy to have them write and amend as necessary).

Let's go back to John's test taking. His Strategy Card could look like Figure 6.1.

Figure 6.1 John's Strategy Card for High-Stakes Tests

	Sequence	Precision	Technical Reasoning	Confluence
Your LCI Scores	28	15	25	23
Your Description of Your Learning Patterns				
How do you "naturally" use each of your Learning Processes?	I'm organized. I break my work into steps. I check my work to make sure that I'm following the directions.	I don't ask many questions. I don't read much either. I can find facts when I need to, but I don't use big words, and I hate writting.	What is the purpose of learning this? How will I ever use it? Let me get my hands on something real and fix it or make it work.	I have some ideas that connect to what I read and that I can use for my writing, but I am not into taking risks!
Your Analysis of the Learning Patterns Needed to Complete The Task (See the Decoded Task Directions)				
What does the assigned task require each of your Learning Processes to do?	I must read and follow directions carefully. I will only have a certain amount of time to do each section of the test.	I will be asked to read and find facts to support what I write. Help!	The test is asking me to show that I understand what I've read or listened to.	This test won't ask me to imagine or do really unusal things.
Your Strategies for Using Your Learning Patterns Most Effectively				
How can you Forge, Intensify, or Tether your Learning Processes to complete the tast successfully?	TETHER so I have enough time to write my answers. I will check my work at the end.	FORGE by reading the passage like a detective looking for facts that I can use to write about and make my point.	TETHER so that I don't keep demanding relevance. Just do it and get the job done!	USE AS NEEDED I need to answer the questions and use ideas that are in the reading passage not make up my own.

Conferring With Students About
Strategy Cards: Walking the Walk Ourselves

It's important for students to discuss their Strategy Cards with others. It reaffirms the intention behind developing one and helps to give learners insights about the variety of strategies available for success. FITing our Patterns is not easy! Making a Strategy Card does not guarantee success. It requires discipline, effort, and encouragement to remain intentional.

Making and sharing my Strategy Card with students heightened my awareness of how challenging it is to change behaviors and attitudes. Major change requires constant tending at first. It is hard to give up familiar ways, even when they aren't optimal means of accomplishing a task.

My advice to teachers is to walk the walk yourself. "Go first!" Prepare and model your Strategy Cards; show your engagement in what you're asking of student learners. Don't stand back and watch others prepare to mount personal obstacles they've publicly identified. Making, modeling, and using your Strategy Cards makes you more empathetic toward the challenge of changing your natural Pattern use. More important is the experience it provides you in helping student-learners take the plunge themselves. This implementation activity is central to moving students to active engagement in their learning.

LML's Effect on Student
Engagement (Bob's Perspective)

As Bonnie's kids say, this chapter is huge. Her classroom has reached the point where kids must decide whether to go on to be *learners* (in LML terms) or remain at the stay-and-play stage as *students* (preLML school acculturation). Choosing the former course puts them in Bonnie's situation, wrestling to break free from old, imposed ways of thinking, doing, and feeling. In doing so, they will experience some of the internal tension Bonnie feels. This is also where kids immersing themselves in LML break away from whatever value they find in multiple intelligences and learning styles, as their teachers do, because these don't go where LML takes learners who move on from being mere students.

> Kids must decide whether to go on to be *learners* (in LML terms) or remain at the stay-and-play stage as *students* (preLML school acculturation).

Bonnie's Experience
of Change (Bob's Perspective)

Bonnie's analysis is a window into how deeply her students are acculturated into the tacit assumptions of the schooling she struggles to escape. Central to following Bonnie's lead is their need to move from passivity assigned to them by schooling assumptions (teachers do and decide, students accept) to action for intentional and responsible learning. Bonnie infers that some kids await the unveiling of the *secret of Pattern hierarchy* aligned with assumptions of good/bad categories. Others suspect LML will "pin them down . . . for someone else's convenience." Perhaps they are passively awaiting coercion. Few anticipate that LML, rather than "making them do things," will allow, equip, and liberate them to do more and better learning by taking charge of it themselves. Why no anticipation? There is no experience in their schooling that anticipates it. Bonnie's reflection demonstrates how far she's liberated herself from the grasp of traditional schooling acculturation.

The challenge to consider becoming an intentional learner comes from a kid with the courage to externalize her internal talk: "So, what's the point?" Once opened, the validity question precipitates a flood of other questions that move implementation farther. Are my LCI scores valid? If I don't like my Patterns, can I change them? Is a higher score a better score? To embed LML deeply in the self, the intentional learner-to-be must accept the validity of the following propositions: Validly established Pattern scores are immutable (but can be adjusted temporarily by using the tools of FIT), and higher scores are not better scores; accepting and understanding how my valid scores authentically represent *me* as a learner is necessary for moving to higher levels of learner functioning (metacognition and Intentional Learning).

As Silverberg's study (2002) showed, understanding oneself as a learner is the necessary gate everyone, student or teacher, must pass through to become an intentional learner. The amazing thing is that all learners—different as they are, with unique Learning Patterns— are equipped to grasp this central meaning.

This chapter is also huge because its implementation activities provide all the learning tools necessary to progress from the gate to Intentional Learning. Task analysis provides the equivalent in understanding a task to what LCI scores provide about understanding a person. Task analysis lets us figure out what the context, process, problem, or test we confront requires of us to perform well. The concept tools—FIT—provide means for adjusting our Patterns in intentional, temporary ways to create Pattern FIT with the understood task. The tool volume supports understanding of our learning and that of others. The Strategy Card integrates other tools and presents the big message: You are in charge of your own learning. It describes the learner in general terms; it contains task analysis for a particular task; it contains self-designed specific strategies for accomplishing the particular task. As a total tool and metacognitive crib sheet, the Strategy Card reminds you how to create a best FIT between you and a particular task. As a set, these are powerful liberating tools—and kids in third grade master them easily.

What personal and professional challenges have you faced when seeking to implement change in your school or classroom? How do your experiences help you to identify with Bonnie's?

7

February

Learning to Navigate
the Challenges of Group Work

Vignette: Anything but the Goat

Russell's group was more than ready to vote him off the collective island. The kids were gathered around a group table.

"You don't get what it's like to be working with someone who keeps wandering off!"

"We need him to stay here with us!"

The girls banded together in anger at him. "He doesn't listen to us! He doesn't follow directions! He's so annoying! We can't get him to do anything!" His team members were steely-eyed standing before me. They'd happily have barbecued him if I'd allowed it. Russell (S27 P26 T25 C22) was sitting at his desk, head down, working on something. He didn't appear to interact with his group at all.

"He doesn't want to be any of the fable parts in our Aesop skit."

Russell spoke up for the first time. "That's not true. I just don't want to be the goat!"

"But we asked you what you wanted to be and you wouldn't answer!" Russell looked at me.

I looked through their Group Covenant—Maura (S19 P19 T24 C24), Dina (S19 P17 T25 C22), and Lucy (S29 P24 T20 C26)—and reviewed what members said they needed when they selected one another for the Aesop unit. I remember telling them about having a Strong-willed Learner among them, he being the only boy. I anticipated that, being strong-willed, he might take charge; they needed to avoid coding it as strictly a girl/boy issue. The girls were ready to excoriate Russell. They felt he was just doing his own thing. They needed him but couldn't get him to make decisions about their coming performance. There was a communication breakdown; they were mired. (See Figure 7.1 for a visual representation of the Pattern conflict occurring in this vignette.)

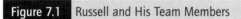

Figure 7.1   Russell and His Team Members

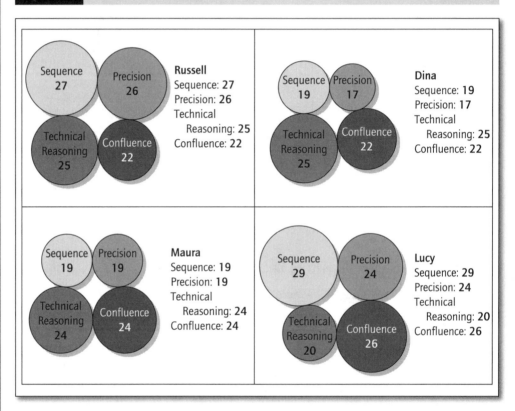

What happens in Russell's group in the vignette happens in many groups. Kids join together, set a plan for action, and experience frustration when things don't go smoothly. They each bring different expectations and skills to group work. Unless they know what those are and can address them head on, they often repeat negative past group experiences. This was a teachable moment.

I could feel the sense of disconnect among them. I turned away from the girls and sat next to Russell, thinking it best to direct my commentary to him, not them. They were wound up, frustrated. Perhaps the way to get the girls to listen was to let them overhear my conversation with Russell, which I worked to keep descriptive and nonjudgmental. I'll use the fishbowl technique without announcing it and see where it goes.

I turned to Russell, "It's hard to be a Strong-willed Learner in a group unlike us, isn't it? You and I don't feel we need a group to begin with. When we could probably do all the work ourselves, it's hard to feel that a group is going to do much for us." I shrugged, remembering that yesterday Russell had taken initiative quickly to help the whole class get the homework assignment. He neither needed nor asked for permission. He was about helping others. I wasn't surprised.

"Sometimes the groups we're in aren't much fun for us. We have to work so hard at Tethering our Patterns."

Now, I'm aware of the girls again; I can feel them still glowering at Russell and, by default, at me. How annoying I must seem to them; they felt themselves the truly injured party, and I'm not taking care of them because I'm not agreeing with them. What's worse, it appears I'm trying to problem solve with him, even appearing to side with him, the root of the group conflict.

"I always find the hardest part of being in a group is waiting for others to understand what I get right away. I can usually see a result at the very beginning because I make plans quickly, and the rest of the time is trying to convince others of my plans."

"That's right! All the girls want to do is talk about this and talk about that, and they don't make a decision that sticks. That bothers me," Russell admitted.

The girls exchanged a look but said nothing. It's one thing to think about how people learn and respond differently when it's just theoretical. But when those differences begin to manifest themselves, initial strengths can feel like obstacles instead.

*I reminded them that their Covenant stated they would figure out inevitable group problems based on their learning differences. How were they different? How could they, **F**orge, **I**ntensify, or **T**ether (FIT) their Patterns to accommodate others?*

I continued with Russell, sensing from the group's demeanor that we had turned a corner.

"We're independent and capable enough to work alone very happily. We usually don't need the group's opinions—we have our own plan of action. Waiting for the group to decide makes us feel restless. We can become fed up and just remove ourselves before others figure out we're not happy. They miss all the signs that we're already 'gone' so to speak, even when we're still there."

I'm speaking for him, I know, but the girls are listening, so I am trying to get them to see what I think is happening.

"I need to use words to let the group know what I need because I rarely look like I need anything, ever. You and I are pretty self-sufficient. We rarely look like we're mad or upset, so people can't read us well. It's hard for them to figure out how to help us unless we have a strategy in place to handle this. There's a gap there, and it's hard to close."

"Yup, that's me."

"You need to stay with your group. Consider other people's ideas as they come up. Don't remove yourself. If you just leave, then they don't have you— they don't have your Patterns—which they need. If you leave, you don't have their Patterns, and you don't learn from them." I read the Group Covenant aloud to them once again, read what they each said they wanted and needed from one another. I saw sheepish smiles.

> "So Russell, you need to Tether your Technical Reasoning, tell the group what you need and keep the compromise in mind. They have to Forge or Intensify their Sequence and Precision so you don't either just take over making the plans or just walk away."
>
> I looked over their Patterns and noticed that Dina's (S19 P17 T25 C22) Sequence and Confluence were in the Use As Needed range (18–24), so she could be more flexible about considering another emergent plan of action, with different details.
>
> "Dina, we need your help here. This is what we call a Pattern conflict. It's not a boy-girl thing and not a personality thing. Russell's high Technical Reasoning, Sequence, and Precision in combination make it hard for him to keep processing decisions as they keep evolving: He had a plan already. Maybe you can help the group consider some other options."
>
> Later, as the group worked together on an Aesop's fable involving a goat, the girls asked Russell what part he wanted, and he said, "Anything but the goat! I don't want the part of the goat, but I'll do anything else. Anything," he assured his group. It was agreed, and they negotiated a different plan. I checked in on them a little later. The group was laughing a bit over someone's funny sound effects, and for now, they had regained a footing. They resolved a Pattern conflict successfully and gained appreciation for their learning differences. And Russell was not the goat on several levels.

Bonnie's Reflection on Russell and the Group

Resolving the inevitable challenges of group work is always problematic. I am usually called to be judge and jury, to dispense a solution after ascertaining guilt, and to prop the group up until the next problem. I understand why teachers find group work tiring and frustrating. In the past, I never found a system or idea that worked satisfactorily. Inservice workshops and class management articles I found wanting. Creating groups by sorting or diversifying using friendships, interests, familiarity, skills, or gender as criteria made little difference or sense. Strategies for resolving differences were illusive. My standard advice for improving interaction, "Just be nice to one another," was a commentary on the civility I wanted kids to extend to one another, not practical help.

Yet I always believed group exercises were important. Looking to the future, one large goal I had was preparing my students for jobs in our society. Working in isolation isn't adequate preparation for whatever is coming. At minimum, the future will require them to be effective in interacting and negotiating with one another as a foundation for problem finding and solving. I was, again, frustrated, lacking knowledge and ability to facilitate student achievement in this important sphere of interpersonal interaction and task accomplishment.

In the past, I would not have spent much time debriefing group problems with the kids. I'd be concerned about them just being nicer and moving on to the work, thinking that debriefing was time off task and getting the job done was the objective. Now, I understand that using Let Me Learn (LML) language depersonalizes the sting of conflict and gives kids time to calm down and reflect on what is happening within them and others. Debriefing gives them space to consider new possibilities and tools to resume their efforts, so time spent on problem framing wasn't lost. Debriefing with Russell and the group reinforced a message that learners working in groups need to hear at the time of the conflict: Others aren't intentionally being difficult simply to annoy us.

Group work elicited the greatest use of the LML vocabulary because projects assigned to students at this time of year were more complex and necessitated more task analysis, more need to Tether, Forge, or Intensify individuals' Pattern use, and more need to communicate and negotiate work plans. Before using LML, students were unaccustomed to thinking about what might be advantageous for task completion. Most kids reported simply picking friends. I suggested thinking of group work as "hiring out your Patterns" to others.

> I suggested thinking of group work as "hiring out your Patterns" to others.

For some kids, thinking of themselves as value added produced the greatest shift of attitude and affect. They needn't be the smartest or the most popular in this new interactional environment. What a relief. They could just be themselves. I made them confer with me at first so that they demonstrated their rationales for making the selections they did before they wrote up Group Covenants, committed to a group, and signed their intentions to remain as a group.

At first, signing a Covenant seemed novel and dramatic; it was accompanied by some giggling. However, when inevitable challenges arose and kids wanted to quit, I wouldn't release them from their commitments. "What do you mean I can't start over with another group? They're annoying. I don't want to work with them anymore." When we talked about how we bring ourselves wherever we go, how challenges experienced aren't isolated events but results of how we think about others and ourselves, and how we're likely to keep running into the same issues with different people, it gave some students pause.

Group selection became its own curricular objective. We spent much time talking about challenges, strategies, and successes. There was much laughter as learners shared the ups and downs of working cooperatively and some poignant moments as well, as learners recognized they had the power to reconcile differences and move on. Many previously had the experience of only conflict and had walked away after being rescued believing that working with others was just too difficult.

I appreciated that after the conversation with Russell and his group they continued to work through challenges to find win-win solutions themselves. To their credit, they reworked the problem through a learner-oriented lens, and brought themselves back to the table.

Implementation Activities

Transition to Group Work: Debunking Old Myths About Working With Others

To initiate effective group work, learners need to understand how their Patterns are intertwined in all learning experiences. They must gain awareness of what they need from groups as well as what they bring to the group experiences so that each member understands his or her value added. Learners need an experiential understanding of Pattern interplay as it informs their interactions with others—how working with others affects their thinking, their work processes, and their feeling about the experience.

I observed how students with different Pattern strengths experienced frustrations with groups. Those leading with Use First Sequence often complained about how someone changed the agreed upon plan, or worse, refused to make a plan. Learners with strong Use First Technical Reasoning leads often got antsy with lots of planning and talking; they wanted to do things or took off physically and did their thinking while wandering around. Those with Use First Confluence liked to keep generating new and, they thought, better ideas or ways to do things, which irked those wanting to plan and stay with it. Learners bringing Use First Precision leads into a group wanted many facts and sometimes kept trying to prove they were right about small issues. Strong-willed Learners frequently developed individual plans and had difficulty yielding to others' ideas. I needed to help all of these learners recognize how Patterns were affecting how they behaved and felt about group work and how to learn to make positive use of the learning diversity in their groups.

Developing Group Covenants: Hiring Out and Borrowing Learning Patterns

The Aesop shadow puppet unit is my most involved and interactive unit. Students research and design a presentation about Aesop, the Greek storyteller. They read and analyze 20 of his fables, select one fable to perform, gather multiple versions of the chosen fable, generate a collaborative script incorporating various fable versions, give parts to all group members, design and create shadow puppets and scenery, rehearse, and finally present their adaptation to a live audience. All Learning Patterns are needed and used interchangeably in the researching, reading, writing, creating, and performing cycles. I laid out the cycle of tasks within the unit. This year, we together examined the Patterns required to undertake these varied tasks effectively.

I asked the kids to think about their Learning Connections Inventory (LCI) scores in relationship with other prospective group members. I distributed a sample Group Covenant (See Figure 7.2) on which students were asked to identify each prospective team member by LCI Patterns and note the most significant aspects about each person's Learning Patterns. Students were asked to identify how they could help the group to be successful and what in turn they required from the group, having analyzed the tasks at hand and what other Pattern combinations they needed to be successful. Each member signed off on the agreement to work together. Their agreement constituted their promise to work and remain together.

| Figure 7.2 | A Sample Covenant |

Curt will bring his Sequence to the group and help Jane and Kate Intensify their Sequence and be more organized with their thoughts. He will also hold onto all of the papers so we don't lose anything.

Kate will help Christine Forge her Technical Reasoning when working on something that has a lot of parts and problem solving. Jane will make sure to help Curt understand what Kate is doing by asking Kate questions like, "What are you doing?" and "How does that work?"

Jane will help Curt and Kate Forge their Confluence when they have to take new risks and come up with unique ideas. Curt and Kate will help to make sure that Jane stays with just one idea the whole time and not get off task.

I gave class members time to mull over whom they thought were good matches for them given the class Profile. From experience and task complexity, I felt that groups of four were ideal: There was enough writing for each child to do; every student must participate in the performance, and every student must contribute to the group presentation on Aesop. Given the inevitable illness absences or music lessons and other pullouts, teams of four could still function reasonably with a temporarily absent partner.

Everyone Has Value Added: Looking at Learners, Not Just Classmates

Group selection generated interesting class dynamics; everybody had value added. It took some a while to recognize how advantageous their Patterns could be for a group. It was interesting to watch degrees of initiative taken. Some kids stood waiting to be selected by others and looked to me for help when no one asked them. Others ventured forth with a plan in mind about where and with whom they wanted to work, calling out, "I'm Technical and Sequential! I'm good at organizing!" Some students wanted to legislate who couldn't work with others or who wouldn't be allowed in to the group, only to be outvoted on new terms. "I don't want us to work with so-and-so." "Well, I do, so I'll take him in my group." I saw evidence of the old social hierarchy attempting to assert itself—but not generating much traction. The kids were looking at LCI charts and using scores to navigate among classmates as the primary sorting criterion.

Some students started groups of their own and hired others whose Patterns were necessary to complement theirs. Some required greater prompting than others to solicit prospective group members. However, students whose Patterns were hired felt good about themselves, and no one was left out.

Forming and Sustaining Effective Groups

As class assignments become more complex over the year, students increasingly need to work with others to shoulder ideas and share work responsibilities. Many of the study units take several weeks to complete, so it's important for students to enter into each group selection process thoughtfully because groups are formed and sustained for the duration of the unit.

Prior to group selection, we engage in task analysis. It's imperative for learners to understand what is being asked of their group in the unit ahead, so they can consider what Learning Patterns are required and anticipate the Profile of the cooperative group they must form to be successful in applying their combined tools to the task. I provide ample class time for this. Students need time to mull over their ideas, confer with colleagues, and make their group selections using the class LCI charts to determine whose Patterns, in what combination, provide the greatest complement to their own. Group selection allows learners to hire out their Patterns and borrow others' as they need. When the unit ends, groups evaluate their experiences, offer themselves and others advice for the future, and disband to form new groups. We continue in this cycle to the end of the year.

Students ask me if there's a perfect number for a group. My answer is no less than three, no more than four. However, what is more important is that learners understand how they add value to the group they're in and how each individual has pledged commitment to the group's success.

Community Support for Learners

Once students sign a Group Covenant, I consider it binding and do not release them from it. However, we don't enter into it quickly or haphazardly. They have to pitch justifications for choosing one another. They need to make informed choices about ways they will contribute to the group and to make their expectations clear. A simple way for students to frame the selection of group members is to have them consider what each brings to the group and what each needs from the group in return.

> A simple way for students to frame the selection of group members is to have them consider what each brings to the group and what each needs from the group in return.

There's an important ebb and flow so that each individual feels valued. Once the group discusses what they need, given their Pattern combinations, and states what they can offer one another, they fill out their Covenant and sign their names. I, too, sign their Covenant, a seal of commitment from one and all.

Anticipating Challenges: Pattern Conflicts Will Occur

We anticipate challenges inherent in the group's construction and lay them out before work begins. Guiding discussion questions include the following:

- What Patterns are in the Use First range? In how many members?
- Who among the group has Avoid Patterns? Which ones?
- Is there a Bridge Learner in the group (Use As Needed for all four Patterns)?
- What strategies do you have to handle challenges when they arise?
- What contribution do you personally make to the group?
- What support do you need from the group?

Strong-Willed Learners

Strong-willed Learners do tasks using three or four Use First Patterns and are their own "team of one." They have difficulty compromising because they can succeed alone, yet they need group process experience to learn how to let others support them, to offer their skills to others, and to learn to negotiate effectively with others. Strong-willed Learners need to learn to include others, and other learners need to be more assertive with these sometimes overly confident individuals.

Bridge Learners

Bridge Learners, with all four Patterns in the Use As Needed range, become the glue for many groups because they can adapt easily to the demands of the task and the needs of the group. They are especially helpful, and were named as such, because of their ability to "bridge the gap" between learners whose scores are widely different within the group.

Of course, not every classroom will have enough Dynamic and Bridge Learners to be able to balance their groups. In those cases, the group needs to take into consideration what Patterns they are missing and discuss in their Covenant how the group will address that missing balance.

Helping Mark and Kira Work Together Optimally

Suppose Mark (S22 P32 T17 C23), a learner who leads with Use First Precision, wants to work on a research project with Kira

(S29 P10 T28 C30) because he recognizes the project requires significant Sequence, and Kira's Sequence is Use First. However, Mark notices that Kira and he are opposites on Precision: She Avoids (very low volume of 10) while he is high Use First (high volume of 32). Their extreme scores don't balance out like an average in math. More likely, they will drive each other nuts because their minds are naturally attending to very different, but important, aspects of the research project. Their differences show up when they try to do research together. Mark's strong Precision has him highly focused on getting all the facts, proving the information he knows, taking careful notes, and getting it right. Kira with her Avoid Precision simply isn't interested in facts, notes, and perfection. Her high Sequence is talking to her about getting organized, making an outline, a plan, and working through it step-by-step. He'll think Kira's going too fast, missing key facts, making an outline before she knows what goes in it, and drawing conclusions before he even knows the details. She'll think he's beating a dead horse, drowning them both in details and words when he ought to be concerned about an outline, a plan.

Pattern Conflicts

Mark and Kira's inherent Pattern differences create a Pattern conflict because their scores (revealing attitudes, approaches, thinking, and feelings) about specificity and facts are extremely different. Mark and Kira understand they need a third individual, whose Precision score Bridges theirs—one higher than Kira's and lower than Mark's—someone able to be a buffer and translator/communicator between their two extremes. Mark recognizes that Tethering his Precision over a long period is highly frustrating. Kira, too, understands that constantly Forging her Precision is tiring. They enlist a Bridge Learner, Jonathan (S23 P21 T22 C19), who joins the group. All four of Jonathan's Patterns are Use As Needed, which complements the group's Profile. Jonathan moderates the two extreme voices between Mark's Use First Precision, "This is so important to include!" and Kira's Avoid, "This is so not! It's way too much information!"

In the heat of the moment, it's hard to remain calm when a group member angers or frustrates us, as Russell and his group revealed. Mark and Kira know they have to anticipate difficulties, even as friends who respect each other. There is no intention behind their experience of Pattern conflict, an unintentional negative interaction resulting from their pronounced Pattern differences. The conflict is generated because of their lack of explicit communication concerning their differences in how each approaches learning. Most interactional difficulties are at heart, Pattern conflicts. There are effective solutions for them if learners are aware of the origin of these conflicts, aware of the reasons they appear, and remember they are not intentional. Unfortunately, those who don't have LML to explain Pattern conflict for what it is typically resort to attributing nasty intent to the other person(s) in the conflict. We saw this very well in Russell's group vignette.

Helping students navigate inevitable interactional challenges arising from Pattern conflict is not easy, but there is a process and a tool to support students in developing and maintaining civil work groups in which learning occurs: the Group Covenant.

LML's Effect on Pattern Conflicts (Bob's Perspective)

In the group conflict vignette and Bonnie's reflection, we see one very practical reason for implementing LML—identifying and dealing effectively with Learning Pattern conflicts. LML defines Pattern conflict as unintentional negative interaction of individuals because of pronounced Pattern differences or conflict generated because of individuals' lack of communication concerning their differences in learning. As Bonnie anticipated, conflict erupted in the group of three girls and one boy, a Strong-willed Learner. Russell retreated as they heaped blame and anger on him. Boom! A cycle of unending blame ensued, and productive group work ended.

Recall from Chapter 3 Jordan's puzzle about the "list of all the good kids" and how students not on that list are not valued by teachers. Kottkamp and Silverberg (1999) studied this phenomenon, finding that teachers often marginalize, isolate physically and psychologically, "problematic" kids. One conclusion was that Learning Pattern conflicts are highly related to teachers' perceptions of problematic behaviors and subsequent marginalization of children. Unrecognized systemic Pattern conflict operates in most classrooms; the elephant in the room predictably stomps on some kids and avoids others.

Testing is another venue of unrecognized Pattern conflict. In Chapter 6, Bonnie describes the implementation activity, "Simulating John's Internal Talk During a Test," a student's preparation for the English Language Arts assessment. Bonnie's focus is purposeful, for tests contain systemic Pattern bias advantaging learners on the dimensions of Sequence and Precision while disadvantaging learners high in Technical Reasoning and Confluence. In a study of high-stakes testing, past test examples, rationales, and grading rubrics for writing tests administered in a dozen states were retrieved from state education Web sites (Kottkamp, 2006). Task analysis found Pattern bias. By far, the most required Pattern was Sequence followed by Precision; Confluence was sometimes in evidence in the test prompt but never in the invariant grading rubric, producing a bait-and-switch situation for learners leading with this Pattern. Technical Reasoning was simply absent. So consistent is the systemic Pattern conflict structured into schooling that knowledge of Pattern scores predicts academic performance in a Sequence/Precision-oriented curriculum and assessment system.

> So consistent is the systemic Pattern conflict structured into schooling that knowledge of Pattern scores predicts academic performance in a Sequence/Precision-oriented curriculum and assessment system.

The worst-case Pattern conflict is a child who leads with Technical Reasoning and Avoids Precision. Very few of these learners graduate with a healthy sense of themselves as learners; instead, they leave school out of frustration or boredom, or they graduate having spent the majority of their years incorrectly identified as having a specific learning disability or SLD (C. Johnston, 2003).

LML's Effects on Resolving Pattern Conflict and Building Teams (Bob's Perspective)

LML's ability to uncover Pattern conflict is important; it allows students and teachers alike to reduce or prevent baleful consequences. But recognizing Pattern conflict is not alone sufficient. There is much to learn from the way Bonnie takes action. Three aggrieved girls demand she act as judge and jury. They are caught up in a self-fueling cycle of prescriptive, judgmental language rendering them incapable of listening. Bonnie speaks to Russell only in descriptive, fact-oriented, nonpejorative terms, using the LML vocabulary in real-time descriptions. She also uses self-disclosure. Her behaviors break the cycle, slow the action, and enable all present to enter into listening mode, as she provides data about the situation. Thus, LML provides critical tools, important skills, and a lexicon by which to communicate, but it takes a wise, intentional teacher to employ the lexicon descriptively, to reduce emotional upset, and to allow reflection to be applied to group functioning.

How important is LML's application in improving group functioning? The evolving global economy increasingly requires employees to work effectively in small groups while our education system remains heavily weighted toward individual performance and outcomes. A professor in an MBA program and later educational leadership at Adelphi University, Patricia Marcellino (2001) employed LML in a research agenda on understanding and improving team function among graduate students in business and education. Her work demonstrates that using LML with fidelity improves group functioning. By providing practical group work skills through LML in sixth grade, Bonnie is moving students far ahead of the preparation curve for future employment.

Can you imagine group work in your classroom or in faculty meetings being practical and effective when those present are intentional learners?

8

March

The Tipping Point

March was the crux of the implementation for me. I finally asked *myself* the difficult question: "Why am I doing this?" My students recognized back in January that they were going to the junior high, a place not familiar with the Let Me Learn (LML) Process and wondered aloud what the point was of learning about learning at such a juncture in their lives. But it took me until March to reach the questioning some of them expressed months earlier.

Vignette: An Internal Crisis

March has always been my intensely introspective month of accountability. March signals the school year will end quickly, and I still have much to share yet with my learners before they graduate. I feel anxiety rising. Two-thirds of the curricular year is completed and my focus always turns to intentionality, both students' in learning and mine in learning and teaching. It's the moment of reconciling what I had hoped for and what I actually achieved. Did Brian make progress in writing? Is Austin reading better after all the morning sessions? How's Kippy's organization? Is Courtney solving problems any differently? I always have a long list of tracked items. This year, I added the implementation of LML.

I process my personal accountability with a close colleague, Simone. She listens as I share the scrutiny of the war I am currently waging within myself.

> *She acknowledges my struggles and gives her perspective on what she thinks I do as a teacher and what I value. She adds her insights about the implementation and the effect on the kids. "I get what you're doing. I understand it now. You've taught the kids that they each have value added as learners, and you hold them to that when they come to the table."*

My Precision Pattern Intertwines With Accountability and Outcomes

I have high standards for others, higher for myself. I'm hard on myself. I say I don't believe in perfection, but I sure catch myself striving for it. This is a major tension my Precision sustains.

The Strong-willed Learner I am exacerbates this tension. In my teaching practice, it knuckles me under every time I forget that I am not the hub of the instructional wheel. I am not the prime mover of the students' learning. I am not in charge of everything. I cannot control every outcome. I lose sight of this in March. I must remind myself of the learners' responsibilities to themselves. I don't own their learning; I facilitate it.

I know the tension intellectually, but I must keep overcoming it every time it emerges. The affective fallout is disappointment with being unable to reconcile the tension once and for all. On the one hand, I am the teacher. I can't share responsibility with others or yield to the learners. My job is to teach students. I am in charge. I am held accountable for whether the students flourish, flag, or tread water on my watch. I am the responsible party. It's my name next to the accountability box that is checked off. Name equals reputation. Teacher equals my self-identity. That's my professional math. As a teacher, I confront my worst fears: I haven't done enough or well enough. I haven't done it perfectly.

Transition Issues: On to Seventh Grade

My learners will be moving on in a few weeks, without me, to the junior high school. The truth is, for this group, their best academic days are happening right now. I am indeed worried for them going to a new, nonLML-aware school environment. At the same time, I don't want to foreshorten the happy days we are experiencing by focusing on some indefinite time ahead, when I am still very much engaged in the present.

The future, in my more pessimistic estimations, is a return to their past: another nonLML school environment experience. The kids'

January reservations were valid, to a great extent. Nobody in our district knows much about the LML Process.

In light of the students' future, I have a sense of foreboding, and I question our progress and myself.

My Assessment

I resolve to get feedback on my concerns. I e-mail my LML friends and make phone calls to my dissertation committee members. I start asking for fresh insights from those who I know have implemented LML to a far greater degree than I have. Fortunately, help arrives, not as I had anticipated in one dramatic swoop but in waves.

A late winter ice storm arrives unexpectedly, and my computer service is temporarily suspended—not the inconvenience I would ordinarily think but a much-needed opportunity to get out of my sedentary routine, to redirect attention away from my writing, implementation, and e-mail. No sage words will come my way for now. I turn off my laptop and head outside to chip ice instead, as my driveway had become fully encased. One car is entombed, and I have to clear a path to the door. I have an unexpected opportunity to Forge my Technical Reasoning, reframe my current dilemma, and consider some practical solutions.

Mulling, Rehearsing, and Revisiting the Problem Differently

The time outdoors is necessary, not only for the activity at hand but also to give me time to suspend negative thinking and focus on a more tangible, doable task. *Chip. Chip. Shovel. Fling. Repeat.* In getting back to bare ground, the repetitiveness of the ice chipping motion requires no great cognitive ability. Done even imperfectly, it yields a visible result—some ground emerges, a stone, a step. This is the right job for me.

Shoveling and chipping ice reminds me (as my student Martin reminded his colleague back in December) that I have four Patterns at my disposal; two are killing me at present, my Confluence and Precision. My Sequence doesn't seem so relevant to figuring out what is happening and what do about it. Using my Technical Reasoning holds more promise, but I have to attend to it more assiduously. I need more doing and less thinking about doing or I will fall prey to analysis paralysis. The littlest voice, my 10 in Technical Reasoning, the one Pattern that quietly acknowledges, "There's a problem here, but you can fix this," can only be heard when I turn down the volume on my Use First Learning Patterns. Some Patterns have been left in charge for weeks now, blaring away. Chipping ice has been my way for processing what I am grappling with. It becomes my metaphor for reestablishing equilibrium and effective functioning. It is a step toward being receptive to feedback shortly to arrive.

Receiving Feedback From Significant Others

An LML colleague, Sara, registers her opinion immediately. "You have given your children an open door to their learning. Your hard work is not a loss but rather an achievement toward your children's learning and growth. . . . Continue what you have been doing, but be honest with your kids about the reality of their future education."

Another LML teacher-friend, Janice, offers her insights. "The kids have strategies to use whether their future teachers know LML or not. You have given them very valuable tools. They are leaving you with a different understanding of themselves that they will use in the future."

Another from Bob, my dissertation chair: "Your work is not futile. You need a way to reframe. Take notes and reflections on everything you are experiencing. Spring is coming. You are somewhere on the road to it."

Chris's response, "I would like you to write a book about your journey."

Bonnie's Reflection on the Pain of Change

The learning in March was mine. It's important to share the struggle that accompanies hard-won insight. I could not move to the next phase of growth without confronting the immutable fact that my implementation of LML is deeply affected by my Patterns. LML is not teacher proof, as so many programs claim to be. I recognize that my Patterns set me up to feel the anxiety I am experiencing. My Precision at 30, if not Tethered, drives me to seek perfection, to get it all right. It grabs onto any little doubt or inconsistency, turns it inward and hounds me to do better. My 30 Confluence often counteracts these Precision attributes with willingness to take risks and desire to be inventive. But when Confluence is feeling a little weak, Precision can unleash a great deal of self-criticism. My Strong-willed Learning self is used to doing almost anything well and often at the last minute. The sheer magnitude of this implementation and its long duration, however, presents a much greater challenge than my strong-willedness has been accustomed to dealing with. At times, it feels overwhelmed, and I feel less capable because I have much less practice at overcoming obstacles that many learners take as commonplace.

I realize now that each teacher experiences LML implementation differently. Teachers with Use First Sequence and Precision at Use As Needed are more inclined to look for models, steps to follow, and implementation manuals. They are more likely to seek out implementation coaches and authorities. Precision at that level will seek appropriate information but not hound the person with self-critique. Teachers with Use First Confluence and Technical Reasoning have an entirely different implementation experience. Confluence urges invention and risk tolerance. Technical Reasoning gets in with lots of hands-on tinkering to buttress inventiveness, lots of problem solving and just diving in and doing it. There is much less stand back and analyze. Sure, other teachers will feel tensions while implementing LML, but the specific tensions they feel are, in part, determined by who they are as learners. We are each the specific team of Pattern levels we possess; we each have different feelings, ways of performing, and thoughts as we implement the LML Process.

I recognize I need to take initiative to solve this problem. I see my learning most clearly here, in this vignette, when it occurs to me that I must have greater faith in my students' willingness to become more intentional. I must have greater faith in my abilities as an intentional learner and teacher as well. A double lesson.

I was greatly relieved to receive heartfelt and timely feedback from critical friends and mentors. I needed their perspectives and to understand that what I was feeling was a stage in the change process, not a final event. It was the inevitable "pain and growth" stage in my learning. The intensive self-questioning passed and did not return the following year, a sign of having intentionally applied new strategies, as I experienced a different outcome.

Through reflection, I recognize I need to trust that the LML Process is intended to foster capacity and independence among learners. Learners must practice independence; I need to let go enough to enable them to do just that. Learners want to be successful and will work toward their independence. Learning is not what we do to them—it is an interactive process of discovery involving the learner centrally. In a profession that overemphasizes my teaching practice, I still forget sometimes that the learner is the heart of what I do.

> Learners must practice independence; I need to let go enough to enable them to do just that.

Implementation Activities

My focus of this month was on finding ways to grow LML awareness and interest in my school and district. I began to brainstorm ways to spread the word more formally about LML, by using the LML lexicon of terms in official meetings, talking with school and district-wide colleagues, with parents, and even future students who were not yet LML aware.

I identified some key opportunities to acquaint others with the LML Process and generated this list as my multistaged to-do agenda. The following is the list I generated and will likely keep amending over time. In creating this list, I considered key clusters of influential people who might never actually spend time in my room but whose interests in learning and students are still very much allied with mine.

LML Outreach Possibilities: Ideas to Grow Schoolwide Awareness

Enhancing Classroom Connections

- Create a designated space on my teaching E-Board (online, virtual bulletin board) to create links for parents and students to view LML materials presented in class, links to the LML home page (www.letmelearn.org), and access to a virtual gallery of student work products representing intentional Pattern use.
- Visit the LML Facebook page (http://www.facebook.com/pages/Let-Me-Learn/73152409114?v=app_4949752878) to connect with other teachers and organizations using the LML Process.
- Display student projects with learner LCI scores.
- Display my Learning Patterns on the door of my classroom.
- Post periodic online blog questions about learning; for example, students find/report examples of Pattern uses outside of school. Learners can see and respond to one another's thinking. I can also facilitate dialogue among them.
- Have students interview parents about their school and learning experiences.
- Establish a *learner* (versus student) of the month display.
- Videotape student-led book talks. Explore Patterns evident in book characters and author's style. Students recommend books on basis of Pattern appeal.
- Facilitate a focus group: Graduating sixth graders talk about LML Process, learning, intentional Pattern use to upcoming learners.

Establishing and Enhancing Connections to Colleagues

- Visit teacher study groups, collegial circles.
- Meet with the Academic Intervention Service Team: "Classic Problematic Student."
- Present LCI scores, learner portfolios, student work products at articulation meetings.

LML Beyond the Classroom: Home/School Communications

- Use LML language in e-mail/phone correspondence with parents, recommendations for students, conference forms, report cards/progress reports, and newsletters to parents.
- Introduce LML concepts in monthly school-parent curriculum updates.
- Present at Parent-Teacher Organization meetings: Learning at School and at Home.
- Present at other parent leadership meetings (even nonelementary).
- Write excerpts for district newsletter of events: Contact public events coordinator and district photographer.
- Present at board of education meetings.
- Develop learning displays of student work products in public library, central office buildings, high school, and the like, always incorporating LCI scores and Personal Learning Profiles

LML and Change (Bob's Perspective)

March brings Bonnie's annual personal accountability self-check. We are fortunate that Bonnie uncovers her deepest learning; without her honesty, we would miss the essence of movement through the "pain and growth" phase of LML's personal development. For all who move personal development to the "deeply embedded" level, this phase must be traversed.

Bonnie's crisis is set off by interplay between her need to be in control of her students' future and the challenge her students will face using LML in the nonLML familiar junior high. She has created an oasis in her classroom, but the full press of traditional culture is the environment just outside her door: the conveyor belt-like schedule that forces students to stop in the midst of deep learning and the colleagues who thrive on controlling rather than fostering student learning. When an ice storm knocks out computer service and encases the world in ice, it also suspends her frustrating negative thinking and gives pause to her churning mind.

Reflective Practice Lies at the Heart of the LML Process (Bob's Perspective)

Chipping ice becomes Bonnie's metaphor for regaining equilibrium to function more effectively, hearing all four Patterns, which necessitates turning down the volume of the three that blare away all the time. She gets deeper in reflection than ever before.

There is an important point about reflective practice well illustrated in this chapter. Some proponents of reflection define it as simply thinking about past events. A problem with this approach—in Bonnie's term, being intensely introspective—is that it can become an endless cycle going nowhere. We subscribe to the Osterman and Kottkamp (2004) definition of reflective practice as a cycle activated by surprise or recognition of a problem. This perspective's second stage is collection of data, usually from other sources, not simply one's memory or self-interpretation. Data are gathered to look at one's actions or the outcomes of those actions so that they may then be compared with the intentions that lead to the actions.

Bonnie illustrates the process of collecting data from many sources to help her work through a resolution of the tension she confronts. Bonnie has her observational data in vast quantity because she is researching. She sees kids working with intention both in groups and by themselves. So kids' behaviors provide her data.

She also reaches out for feedback from a trusted colleague, LML colleagues, and her academic mentors. The sum of these data provides evidence that Bonnie's actions and their outcomes are moving kids and her along the path of Intentional Learning and taking responsibility for learning. Her twinges about heroic teaching, taking control, and fear for her kids in the coming year are just that, twinges. She is winning the internal war; she is becoming a fully intentional teacher. The pull of tradition and stability is losing its grip. She is moving toward LML-nurtured change.

What are the areas in your teaching life that hold you back from implementing best practices?

9

April

Evidence of a Transformed Classroom Culture

By April, the class has settled into a wonderfully interactive dynamic focused on learning, building potential, and mutual cooperation. What I appreciate most about the class' progress is the degree to which students help to shape the actions of the others, frequently without my direct intervention. I notice students recognizing the strengths and challenges of their classmates and speaking up without reluctance about something they notice in a student's work. Their observations signal respect for one another as learners.

Vignette: Kippy Gets It Because His Peers Get It!

Kippy started out giving his science fair presentation the way he'd begun his Robert Frost presentation back in December. He had his hands in his pockets, and he was facing the blackboard reading information off a page attached to his poster. He rocked back and forth as he spoke and alternately kicked an imaginary something on the wall, first with his left, then with his right foot. His lack of awareness was disarmingly charming at the time but not at all effective for presenting his research.

This time, Kip began his science fair presentation by reading something about the aerodynamics of the paper airplane, again to the blackboard. He began to bop up and down again as he was talking to the poster. Austin looked over at me and raised an eyebrow.

"Kippy, you're doing it again," Kimberly prompted him, half-giggling, half-exasperated.

"What? What am I doing?" he said, turning around, facing the group. He looked down at his pockets and flinched, as if finding his hands in his pockets surprised him.

"Ahhh!" He pulled his hands out and waved them both at the class. The class laughed. However, he smiled, turned back to the board again, put his hands back into his pockets and resumed, droning on again about paper airplanes and wiggling.

"Kippy!" the class yowled at him. He spun around and caught himself, "Hands!" he cried to more laughter from the class, as he removed his hands from his pockets again and flapped them momentarily. The class jumped in right away, as if to catch him from going back into his quirky autopilot presentation mode.

"Kippy, face us!"

"We want to see you! Don't talk to the board! Talk to us!" They offered him advice.

"You're kicking the wall when you're reading!" Patrick said.

"I do that, too, don't feel bad," another voice replied.

Several students offered suggestions. Kippy smiled and took this all in. In 15 seconds, his presentation went from poor to good. He showed the kids how to make an airplane that flew 35 feet. He encouraged the kids, explained the physical components of the plane he displayed, and watched them try, with varying success, to make the plane that he had modeled.

Bonnie's Reflection

Kippy's presentation was part of an annual classroom activity in which each child presented a completed science project to the class in preparation for the upcoming science fair. The purpose was to share with one another what they'd learned by doing the experiment. Students listened to and asked questions about aspects of one another's research in preparation for the bigger event that evening with parents.

Kip (S29 P22 T21 C24) is a Dynamic Learner who leads with Sequence, then Confluence, followed by Precision and Technical Reasoning. The class enjoyed Kippy's ability to multitask during his presentations, but more important, they enjoyed his ability to make corrections and reframe midstream. Besides entertaining the kids, who enjoyed his antics and his lightheartedness, Kippy showed the class that he valued their suggestions and was attempting to be more mindful about his public speaking habits.

The kids could appreciate one another's weaknesses with a little levity. Kippy demonstrated the Learning Process: He took other's public observations and corrections to heart and attempted to put them into practice. That he wasn't able to do it right away underscored that we often function at deep levels of automaticity. We need to be jolted back into a greater awareness of what we are doing. The class was interested in helping him, and their attention and advice giving indicated that.

Implementation Activity: Simulating FIT—Forging, Intensifying, or Tethering

To help students understand how challenging it is to Forge, Intensify, or Tether (FIT), I designed a classroom writing activity, created to reveal those tensions in which I made very specific limitations to the length of the assignment. I pose nightly reading questions to the kids (e.g., How did Ernest Shackleton anticipate his crew's restlessness while the ship *Endurance* was frozen in the ice pack?) In addition, I gave the directive that their response must be exactly six sentences long. Not more. Not less. Exactly six, including a restated question in the answer, details supporting their opinions, and a quote from the text to bolster their thinking. Most kids would need to FIT their Pattern use to fulfill my directions exactly.

Derek (S29 P25 T26 C23) reported trying to ascertain why, knowing my Learning Patterns and the way the assignment was constructed, I valued it. He kept thinking about what I really wanted as a Precision Use-First teacher. The directions confused him; why write only six sentences?

"At first when I heard you say it, I thought it was going to be easy. But when I got home, I realized that you are like a 31 in Precision. So I asked myself, 'Why would she want us to write only six sentences? Why wouldn't she want me to write a lot more?' Then I was confused about what to do because the directions didn't seem right to me."

Students like Derek were trying to reconcile the gap between what I said I valued and what I was doing. The cognitive dissonance he experienced was an impediment to completing the work of writing and feeling satisfied with the result: The teacher expectations didn't seem to match up. What would be the point of trying to Tether, to write fewer words, when he'd assumed I would want to see more?

Derek's statement revealed several things. He knows me as a learner and understands how my learning influences my teaching. I gave the class writing directions that ran counter to my (untethered) inclinations as a learner. Derek didn't think I would value something requiring me to Tether my 30 in Precision, to accept the students' (shorter, briefer) writing. Why would Ms. D. work outside of her comfort zone? Derek was wondering. Would she really expect the kids, then, to do that, too?

Derek exhibits an incredible degree of metaawareness. This learner frequently looked to the horizon and anticipated questions other students wouldn't approach for a long time to come.

LML and Respect (Bob's Perspective)

It's April, springtime. Bonnie and her students enter the "insights and understandings" phase of Let Me Learn (LML) personal development. As we look into the vignette, we see focused listening and observing mixed with a lightness of spirit and fun. Students offer serious, on-point, honest feedback to Kip. We observe a learning community at work communicating effectively and learning from one another.

LML's imprimatur is on this learning community. Students know one another as learners, as both the presenter and voices from the audience demonstrate. Feedback enables the presenter to become reflective about his actions. There is fun but not at anyone's expense. No one is corrected for misbehavior. There is not a hint of disrespect, in fact, quite the opposite; respect is a tacit norm. Studies over the years tell us that adults and kids alike desire honest information and feedback about their performance, but very infrequently do adults or kids get the kind of helpful honesty seen here (Osterman, 1994). What we observe through the vignette is a learning community functioning well, not merely in name.

LML's Effect on Classroom Culture (Bob's Perspective)

The norms and behaviors in Bonnie's classroom at this point differ importantly from classrooms in general. Learners know themselves well. The history of "good/bad" student differentiation has been transformed into an acceptance of the uniqueness of every learner, for "difference is good."

Bonnie, in many small ways, has reduced the traditional power between teacher and students. She is nowhere in the vignette except as the observer and recorder of student interaction. She is not intervening and controlling the ongoing action or hovering over students as they work together, as she earlier admitted were attributes of her teaching in prior years.

The vignette corroborates and extends the mounting evidence that not only are individual students becoming more intentional but also that the interpersonal interactions and the culture of Bonnie's classroom is on a trajectory of continuing transformation. In November, we had surprising evidence of an amazing and emerging ethic of caring; sense of safety; willingness to take reasonable learning risks; and a developing sense of community, of responsibility taken to cocreate a culture in which each individual is valued. In January, we observed the push off toward intentionality and taking responsibility of one's learning. In February, we received a closeup account of extending LML ways from individual learners into groups, to social collectives, of increased initiative taking (seen in choices of group members based on learning rather than friendship) and of willingness to analyze interpersonal conflicts through an LML lens and to solve their own problems. In April, we see learners offering one another substantive feedback on work products and presentations. Bonnie's learners have expanded the underpinnings of trust, safety, listening, and engagement to include honest and useful critique, pervasive civility, and enjoyment of both learning and one another's company. All the evidence of both individual and social growth from November through April serves as a huge countervailing response to Bonnie's self-critique and sense of failure fueled by her untethered Precision during March. The view from April is one of accomplishment and positive continuing transformation and of Intentional Learning expressed individually and collectively.

Throughout this chapter, we are reminded of the transformative nature of the LML Process: Kids are capable of knowing their learning and learning with others using a specialized lexicon and the special tools of intention—metaawareness and metacognition. This transforming culture as observed in Bonnie's classroom is built on the LML assumptions that learners are in charge of their learning, that the teacher is a fellow learner, and that learning differences are not the root of problems but the equippers and building blocks of strength.

Can you imagine your students critiquing one another with a similar degree of insight and civility as you merely observe them at work?

10

May

So Much to Do—So Little Time!
Panic or Picnic

In school, time is an extremely valuable commodity. There is no slow season, no academic downtime. The pace is fast; all days are claimed. Everything presents itself all at once.

For this day in May, the students and I intentionally pushed frenetic everydayness aside, turned down the volume of productivity-driven background noise, and orchestrated a timeless moment as a class community.

Vignette: A Timeless Moment

Monday was our class picnic I had promised. The kids had been working really hard. I was attuned to how tired they were feeling and wanted to acknowledge their sustained efforts. What would they like? What would be fun? How about a picnic? A resounding affirmation, yes! They wanted lunch outside and time to play together. Given the incessant schedule, this was an opportunity to suspend time and recharge our communal batteries.

The kids were excited when they arrived.

"We're having the picnic, right?" Matthew asked first thing.

"Absolutely, today's the day."

The kids scoured for evidence that others had brought supplies. Austin brought soda, Kippy a fruit plate, and Sallie rainbow cookies. It was gratifying to hear reactions, "Oh, I love those!" and "This is going to be fun!" I added my contributions: folding tables, a beach umbrella, nine Hula Hoops, a chocolate fountain, plates, cups, tablecloths, and food. It took twenty minutes to pack the car and a minute and half to unload with all the kids carrying our "cool stuff."

The kids wanted to eat outside together among the benches and beautiful flowering trees. We set up stations for sandwiches and drinks inside, and the kids helped one another assemble the lunches and bring them outside. By the time I arrived, the caravan was already in place, happily settled, and I was very glad the class and I collaborated to fashion this for ourselves. The kids' concern was the time we'd actually have for our communal picnic. In a flash, the "timeless moment" was assigned a number value. I laughed to myself. We live by the clock in academic culture—buses and cars arrive on schedule.

"We have until 2:15, about two and a half hours to eat lunch, relax, play, and be together. We'll end the day with reading and share our chocolate fountain with the other class."

Our picnic attracted lots of visitors and unusual interest. Some knocked on the windows and waved or stopped by crossing the parking lot. We were a curiosity. The office staff admired the food. The lunch aides approved of the beach umbrella and the Hula Hoops. The reason this caught their attention was that we were celebrating our hard work on a Monday. Scheduling a picnic on the first day of the workweek broke an unspoken rule: Mondays established the productivity regimen for the week. We broke tradition; we needed this badly.

Remembering November

"Remember the time we were all reading our wisdom and suffering stories to each other?" Emma reminded the group.

"Yeah, we were all crying as we were telling our stories," Corey said.

"I remember that," Courtney said. "That was the first time we felt really close."

"You didn't cry that day Ms. D. I remember," Mira remarked.

"I did. All the way home in my car. You just didn't see me."

As the conversation moved on, and they talked about other things, I thought it was significant that the kids remembered that November day. This was the second mention by some and the third by others.

But those moments of reflection didn't last long. Kids wanted seconds on food or drinks and needed my keys to get inside the building. I gave them to Kippy.

"You have the power now," I intoned. He grinned and held the keys up for all to see.

Rejoicing in Our Learning Community

I marveled at the 21 people in my homeroom as they played together outside. This moment revealed a fascinating, three-dimensional social scatter gram—who played with whom, for how long, and in what combination. Everybody had a place. Some conducted hula contests; others were shooting hoops, swinging on swings, or had lined up for kickball. Watching them in action, I considered how, as a teacher and a fellow learner in this class community, I've had to learn to yield and let them in. I couldn't possibly be responsible for all the good ideas, all the problem solving, and all the learning that routinely occurred in and out of my room. There was balance here, as each person added something unique to the collective. How diverse a group this was! How amazing it was to witness our extraordinary progress this year. Some of the progress was clearly theirs, some mine.

At times, when I reflected on daunting aspects of my job and the tremendous sense of responsibility I felt as a teacher, I was relieved by my persistence in developing this class differently. At this point, they each knew the frustrating aspects of community life. They routinely came together to help one another and kept intertwining me in the process. We found good ways through many challenges, and the learning process we'd immersed ourselves in together gave us insights and strategies for connecting with and understanding one another. I couldn't be prouder of us as I sat on the grass watching them from under my umbrella. Savor this moment, I reminded myself. It's ours.

At some point, Kimberly ran up from the field. "What time is it?" she asked. I looked at my watch; it was 2:15. The suspended moment had officially ended.

"It's time," I acknowledged.

Nine yard-sale Hula Hoops, an old beach umbrella, 21 children and a teacher, one communally shared meal, and time—sometimes the most memorable experiences are composed of humble ingredients. The immense pleasure the day provided reminded me that this was the respite we needed—the equilibrium we teachers need to advocate, the condition that supports optimal learning.

Suspending customary press-on practices to achieve a greater sense of balance had always been a challenge in my career—I've always been busy meeting job demands. I noticed this year that school pacing and the avalanche of competing commitments, programs, activities, and units was impossible for this group to process without recalibrating their energies. I recognized how vital that was for my class to continue feeling successful, keep working productively, and engaging actively. No time allotted for debriefing and reflection for this group equaled no learning. I'm thankful we didn't miss this experience because we were just too busy. It was truly one of the happiest days of the year.

Bonnie's Reflection

My Confluence gets caught up in the challenge of trying one more thing, one last lesson in pursuit of more, better, and higher. Thus, I frequently imagine more for my class and for myself than I am able to enact. My colleague Simone playfully admonishes me that the last days of the school year are *not* the opportune time to start something new, when I propose what she acknowledges is a wonderfully creative idea. My timing is motivated by ideas, not the calendar. In school, the calendar, however, dictates all.

This tendency became more obvious to me, working with this class whose optimal learning frequently required more, not less, of the valuable commodity of time to process information and construct knowledge. I realize I'm in charge of orchestrating important *time outs* for my students, for carving out balance and rest time amidst the competing barrage of *usuals* and *have-tos*. No one will honor our need to maintain balance unless I do.

Seeing the kids in a context outside of the classroom gave me a perspective I value but rarely witness—to see them as people, not just as students. It was equally important for them to see me, too, as a person and not just their teacher. The daily reading lesson we returned to afterward was unremarkable in contrast to the collective picnic experience we'd just had. The time away to recalibrate our energies was more important than the lesson plan to meet state standards.

Several members of the class recognized something significant was happening in this group experience. They recalled the affectively charged reading lesson that brought them together that November afternoon months ago. They debriefed once again about what transpired as a community earlier in the year. "Why didn't you cry then, too, with us?" Mira asked me.

They were still processing that powerful event, though the environment of the picnic was happy, relaxed, and decidedly different from that November day. We were not in the November context. It felt good to remember the past yet equally good to be engaged in this new moment. I felt an incredible sense of the depth and distance we had traveled since November as a class community, how much we'd learned about ourselves and one another. From my vantage point, on that sunny May afternoon, we were in a very good place to enter into the last few weeks of school.

Implementation Activities

Later in the month, it became evident that we had insufficient time to complete all the units I had designed for the year. I presented the class with the situation. I was ready to do a hard prune and skip one of the annual events, even though I was sad about it.

Students Become Codesigners

We had three units left but time for only two. I explained each to the students: (1) a poetry unit, (2) a history research project about our school, and (3) a debate unit. "Why can't we just do a smaller version of the annual poetry café so that we can still do the other two?" one student wondered. The kids were interested in helping to solve what they understood affected all of us.

Students offered extensive feedback about each event in which they presented, not just watched as in years before. I took their recommendations to heart because we had coplanned the unit and demonstrated as a group that we could cooperate to achieve a goal. The core elements (research, public speaking, and exposure to different poetic forms) remained. I appreciated the class's perspective on their learning, their awareness that we could still accommodate our needs and maintain a high level of engaged performance. We were able to broker a balance that worked for us as an Intentional Teaching-Learning community.

Taking a Global View of the School Year: Student and Teacher Reflections

All teachers keep track of the lessons and units taught each year. As a natural planner (my Use First Sequence), I keep two sets of books. The first is the global yearly plan. Lately, my district committed us to generating online curriculum maps; plotting weekly and monthly progress in scope and sequences; and noting the state standards met, materials used, and links to resources we employed. It's taken several years to compile the details for multiple subject areas, but it serves a good purpose.

My second planner, however, is much more valuable to me. I established it early in my career and continue to rely on it because it has greater use as a teaching tool. It's the "what really happened and what I thought about it" planner. My second book, in which I record assessments about how the unit went, the glitches, the time it took to complete, what materials are ill timed, what minilessons were well received, what units need pruning, and what resource is outdated. It's my curricular retrospective, what I rely on to make adjustments next year. I revisit my backward planner, add insights, record problems, and remind myself of things to consider. The first planner is what I want to have happen, my intentions. I am aware that, given my high Confluence, I have more ideas than I can put into place. I need to counterbalance that, and the second planner, with its detailed accounting, helps me to reflect on my lived experience and how all of the dynamics of the situation came to bear on the outcome of the original plan. The two planners together are also the necessary elements for my reflective practice.

This year, I asked the students to participate in my reflective review process, creating a global picture with me of our year. As always, I ask questions, make lists, and collect data. This year, students engaged in the process with me. Over several weeks, I asked them to reflect on which units worked, which didn't, and which lessons could work better.

I kept our school calendar handy because we frequently flipped back through the months, talking about our time use as conversation ensued. Some conversations emerged from formal class discussions. Others arose spontaneously as students and I stood in line in the cafeteria, walked down the hall together, or talked after school. I am well-known for carrying sticky notes and never being far from a writing implement. So I recorded what the learners reported on the fly and kept the notes with their more formal assessments and reflections in my planner for next year.

The following are examples of questions I asked over time. Some are set primarily in a language arts orientation but worth sharing because, beyond content focus, they ask learners to speak about what they value, need, and notice. Others are useful in any subject.

- What recommendations do you have about the order of language arts units? Here's my rationale for why I did it the way we did. . . . How did that work for you? What months of the year would be best to do . . . ?
- What units were too long? Too short? What do you recommend to alter the pace?
- What language arts or reading lessons really stayed with you? What made them stand out to you?
- What books did you read (personally) that aren't on the required lists but should be?
- What books did we read that you would remove?
- In what ways did I need to help you more as a writer? How do you want to be able to write better?
- Which projects were especially helpful to your learning? Difficult?
- If we could do one more thing, what would it be?
- What were you expecting (hoping) we'd be doing more or less of this year?
- What were your experiences as a group member? What surprised you the most? What were the highs and lows?

Taking the Recommendations to Heart

I remind the kids that their recommendations are important because, truthfully, no one is walking the walk except them. They have an invaluable insider's perspective on our classroom and daily experience that I want to understand. Once kids know that I write down what they think, read their evaluations, comment on them, and follow up with them, they have a lot to say.

However strong my inclination to reach the learners, I need feedback about my teaching, or I will only maintain my assumptions. How did I actually do? I think we're all fine, but how can I be sure? What was it like for the learners in my class to do what I'd asked them to do? Getting authentic feedback from students required establishing groundwork early and building trust so students recognized my sincerity. They now have the capacity to provide descriptive feedback. More important, they've gained ownership of the work we've done together. I have the capacity to listen to and the willingness to integrate their insights.

LML Sets the Stage for Honest Feedback

As a teacher-learner, I guaranteed up front that the classroom environment would remain open so that students felt comfortable giving me their responses. At the outset, I tell all my classes that I can't improve my practice without their help. Their guidance makes the difference. Still, I spend months giving students permission to say to me,

"Ms. D., I couldn't Connect what you said to anything I care about."

"I need more time at the beginning of class, and you sometimes rush me."

"You don't answer my questions with enough detail, and it feels confusing!"

"You wandered off topic when you tried to tell me about. . . ."

"You need to Tether your Confluence and your Precision!"

"You made a plan and didn't follow through on it! I never got a chance to present yesterday, and it made me mad!"

All these voices are learners I have come to trust in a school context that focuses on my teaching but rarely includes children among my mentors.

My student-learners were more than willing to offer their perspectives. They knew they were more than "just students" to me. Based on their recommendation, I rearranged several activity sequences to reduce frenetic activity associated with certain times of year and to insure that we had time to learn well and have fun yet not feel pressured.

> They knew they were more than "just students" to me.

LML's Effect on the Teacher (Bob's Perspective)

By May, Bonnie functions at the "deeply embedded" phase of LML; it is an inextricable part of her thinking and planning for all learning and teaching. The tone of her inner voice is starkly different from its tone during the tense days of March; now, her voice is quieter; the tone is brighter. She still experiences tension, but it is of a different nature. This tension is about time and its use. It's about the difference between making time determinations based on learner needs versus traditional uses that are simply on the calendar or for adult convenience. But Bonnie doesn't experience this conflict as internal war; she treats it as an external source of conflict. At this point, she understands herself thoroughly as a learner.

This day of the picnic is a special one for the kids. But from an analytic perspective, it almost seems that this day, this carved out "timeless moment" within a day, is more special for Bonnie than the kids. The moment provides a space for Bonnie to observe the kids and for the kids to remember the feeling of community established on the amazing day in November when they shared their writing and their feelings.

What are these observations about? Why is the day so special for Bonnie? Validation. She experiences validation of her intentions in undertaking the LML implementation. In the specifically nonacademic picnic setting, she observes the unmistakable marks of what the kids and she have accomplished together over the year. From Bonnie's need to "be in charge and in control" in March, to "coplanning" with the kids in the inner sanctum of curriculum while attending to their Learning Patterns in May, Bonnie has changed herself as intended. Validation.

What mechanisms do you have in place to reflect on your Intentional Teaching practices? Is student-learner input included?

11

June

Note to Self—I Am a Viable Learner

As the June days ticked by, I was thinking about preparing the kids for next September. Thoughts of junior high school, with all the accompanying excitement and trepidation, were a part of many conversations these last weeks. They were thinking about this next step in small and large ways. I wanted them to have something to prompt thinking back on their learning this year. I asked the students to write a letter to themselves, which they would receive in the mail during their first week of junior high school. That way, they could offer themselves advice on their new lives from their current perspective. Of all of the implementation activities I either infused or introduced as stand-alone lessons, this proved to be most effective.

THE ASSIGNMENT: LETTERS TO SELVES

Your last assignment is simple: Write yourself a letter. I will mail it to you on the first Monday after you begin seventh grade. The purpose of this letter is to remind you in a new school that you are a unique learner. You deserve to have teachers who understand you and understand what you need so that you will attain your greatest potential. You know how I feel about that!

(Continued)

(Continued)

Include a description of you as a learner. Use Let Me Learn (LML) terms. You have a language you can speak! Include a description of what you need from your future teachers so that you can be happy and successful in your new school.

Don't forget to date your letter and sign it. It will serve as a memory of this June day. Bring it in first thing tomorrow morning. I'll hold it over the summer and return it in September as a reminder of how special you are and how important your learning is, wherever you go. This will be your first academic gift to yourself in seventh grade.

Students' Advice to Their Future Selves

The student letters show the depth of understanding they had about themselves, their Pattern use, their needs for optimal learning, and their future hopes. I've included some of them here to show a variety of perspectives about learning and self-identity.

STUDENT ONE (S25 P21 T18 C23)

Hi! Welcome to a new year. Right now, I'm excited to go to seventh grade, but I'm also sad. I'm sad to leave my family where I am comfortable, secure and can just be myself. Besides friends, I'm also leaving an amazing group of teachers and staff, who make me feel as if I'm a million dollars. I hope I will feel the same way at the junior high. I need my teachers to be clear and precise about assignments and homework. I also need them to answer my questions. What I liked about this year in English language arts (ELA) is that Ms. Dawkins asked our opinions. I think more teachers should do that. My teachers also need to give reasons for "why" so I can understand the concept more. I like when the teacher puts us into groups. It makes time more enjoyable, and you get to interact with others. I like when teachers teach something important, but I also enjoy when we get to perform or make things such as the Aesop shadow puppets.

I need someone who understands everybody. For example, if a kid is a different learner than they are, don't pounce on them. Different is good. Patience is also needed. For example, if someone is high in Technical and they walk around the room, ignore it and move on. The kid can't help it. My Learning Connections Inventory (LCI) scores are S25, P21, T18, and C23. Just to refresh, this means that my strong voice says that everything needs to be organized and to take notes (Sequence). My second loudest voice says to create with crazy ideas (Confluence). My next voice says to write a medium amount of words and details (Precision). Finally, my last voice says that I don't need to build or take anything apart (Technical). Therefore, when asked to do a project, I would most likely make a poster with bullets for information. If I was asked to build a diorama, I would really need to Forge my Technical. I hope that my future teachers will respond to what my classmates and I have said. I hope they will accept everybody for the type of learner they are and acknowledge that. Good luck!

Of all sixth graders, this student spoke most directly to the need for teachers to recognize student diversity positively and to advocate for learners. She wanted future teachers to show students the relevance of work given to them and to allow individuals to work together on group projects.

STUDENT TWO (S26 P25 T26 C23)

You might think, Oh man, I wrote to myself, but there's a few things you will need to know. (1) Right now, as this letter is being written, you are the kind of girl whose Learning Patterns (S26 P25 T26 C23) reveal that you have to be walked through something for the first time, and that others have to keep their distance when you are trying to do something on your own. You need things to be neat, orderly, and easy to find. If you have a partner, you have a tendency to go steaming mad when they have trouble catching up. Just remember, people are different than you. (2) You need the teachers who understand a kid's school needs and will support you in school. You need someone who is patient and neat, and someone who has a sense of humor. You need someone who you can talk to about anything from school to growing up.

This student understood that group work will be a challenge, a function of her high degree of independence as a Strong-willed Learner. She wanted a teacher to teach the whole child, not just the "school" child.

STUDENT THREE (S26 P25 T18 C17)

Dear myself,

Now that summer is over, you are finished and are in the junior high. I bet you are enjoying your new school. How is it? Remember all the teachers? Do you remember Ms. Dawkins and LCI scores? There is Sequence, Precision, Technical, and Confluence. Sequence means you're organized,

(Continued)

(Continued)

Precision means you're full of details, Technical means you like to investigate things and Confluence means you're creative and imaginative. Your Sequence is a 26 out of 35 and your Precision is a 25 out of 35, so you're going to have to Tether both. Your Technical is an 18, so you usually have to Forge it, and your Confluence is a 17, so you really have to Forge it. Just remember, that with all these Learning Patterns, you are a unique learner.

To learn at the highest potential I possibly can next year, I will need my future teachers to know about me and what I need from them. I will need my teachers to know that I am very organized and try to be as perfect as possible, I don't really try to "invent" and take things apart. I'm not a good brain-stormer or good at being very creative, and most importantly, I always have tons of details and write a lot! This is what your new teachers need to know about you next year, and this is what you could tell them. Have fun in junior high and for the rest of your academic career!

This student addressed the issue of task analysis and reminded herself that by Forging or Tethering certain Patterns, she'll be able to achieve success.

STUDENT FOUR (S28 P17 T26 C17)

Dear future self,

I learn as an individual and have different Learning Patterns than everyone else. In Sequence, I have a 28 which means I use it first and I am organized. I have a 17 in Precision which means it's not such a strong voice and that I'm not as precise. I have a 26 in Technical which means I use it first and that I like hands-on things. Lastly, I have a 17 in Confluence which means it isn't such a strong voice and that ideas don't flow as freely. Next year I would need a teacher who is down to earth. Someone who has a sense of humor and someone I could talk to.

Sincerely,

Present self

This student described his Learning Patterns in terms of *voice* and how, in turn, each process presented itself to him. The influence of his Technical Reasoning makes his letter brief and direct; it is a quick list reminder of all that he knows about himself as a learner. He does not feel the need to record more on paper because he has it well in hand, deeply embedded within his learning self. Someone who doesn't understand the LML Process would miss the degree of insight and understanding behind what is written here.

Bonnie's Reflection

It is fitting to end a story about a learning year with the voices of the learners themselves. The students speak so clearly, in delightfully preadolescent tones, about their learning needs, their future hopes based on their growth this year as intentional learners, and their academic concerns, given what they know about traditional school life. I am amazed at the enthusiasm still evident in their narratives, written during the last days of school, when I would expect energy levels to be flagging. At the same time, I sense their nervousness about going to a new school environment and beginning a new academic chapter. The graduates do not sugarcoat their expectations but speak hopefully, nonetheless.

Given end-of-year time demands, I nearly skipped this letter assignment. We were three days from the end of school, in full graduation practice mode, taking final tests and emptying desks in 90-degree heat. It was clearly *not* the time to do this. And yet it was. I knew it—once I overcame my misgivings that the kids were burnt out on academics and just wanted to finish the year.

Once I started receiving responses and read them, I recognized the power in this activity, beyond their advice to themselves. These letters revealed the footprints of my teaching. I hadn't considered that in the process of writing up the assignment. The letter to self had been designed for them, yet it exposed the depth of our work this year, which gratified me immensely.

I intentionally left off the names of the learners and included their Pattern combinations, not because I didn't want to acknowledge them but because their responses represented the wealth and variety of the collective. It is not practical to share every letter; I wish I could.

What I saw so clearly was their sense of self. Their words, blending the sophistication of the LML language with the vernacular of adolescence, voiced so beautifully the depth of self-awareness they possessed. I appreciated the sunny confidence they radiated at a point of their lives so frequently marked, in contrast, by loss of confidence in self.

In reading these letters, I noticed several things:

- The students used LML language fluently. They spoke about their Pattern combinations and their awareness of interaction among the four Patterns.
- They perceptively anticipated future roadblocks—being a new member in a larger community, feeling out of place, not running with the crowd (being a "Sequential follower," as one learner stated), remaining true to self in a new environment, and interacting with peers who learn differently with greater patience.
- Their letters indicated high metaawareness. These students demonstrated that they understood who they are and what they need. They acknowledged their uniqueness and the need to attend to that uniqueness. They reminded themselves to attend to the inner talk of their Patterns: Which ones take over and make them anxious when misapplied; which ones are to be savored (*"You are flaming high in Sequence and Confluence!"* one learner wrote about herself)? They offered themselves strategies in anticipation of working effectively with others.
- Many students described attributes of teachers they thought would complement their Learning Patterns; quite a few reflected on the interactional expectations they had that teachers will recognize their learning challenges and even support them in their strengths.

In reading their letters, I thought how appreciative I would have been this September to have them come to me with their learner needs expressed so descriptively. The usual forms I receive about incoming students pale by comparison. The forms I routinely receive about new students don't say anything about how children learn, so they don't inform my teaching. I'm glad I gave my students the tools to be able to speak so descriptively of themselves.

What Is It About LML That Enables Change to Succeed? (Bob's Perspective)

This question is the last sentence of analysis from Chapter 2. We asked you to track and answer it as you read and reflected. Here are some of our answers given in cryptic form.

- LML implemented with fidelity requires teachers to become intentional learners and then to move on to become intentional teachers.

> LML implemented with fidelity requires teachers to become intentional learners and then to move on to become intentional teachers.

- LML provides actionable self-understanding applicable directly to the work of learning and the work of teaching.
- LML shifts emphasis from teaching to learning; it makes this possible by supplying a theory to explain learning, a set of tools, an array of skills, and a lexicon that together enable even young learners to take control of and responsibility for their learning.
- LML advocates and supports shared knowledge of unique individual learners and shared individual responsibility for learning.
- LML provides a theory and concept-grounded lexicon that makes possible publicly shared discussion of internal Learning Processes and experiences in real time.
- LML recognizes and provides description and explanatory theory for the greatest unrecognized source of diversity in most classrooms: Learning Patterns. It makes understanding and working with this form of diversity possible and positive.
- LML alters thinking and communication; it provides previously unavailable theory and concepts; it alters student-student, teacher-student, teacher-teacher, teacher-parent, and student-parent communication by providing all with a shared, non-prescriptive (and more democratic) basis for discussion of learning.
- LML provides accessible learning tools with visible outcomes that provide support for real-time discussion of learning and learning strategies.
- When implemented with fidelity, LML is absolutely child/learner centered: Internal teacher conflicts signal encroachment of traditional schooling practices.
- LML honors and supports constructivist learning philosophy and adult learning theory.
- LML provides learning-based explanations to replace untested assumptions and attributions that have often resulted in harm to learners, such as interpersonal conflict and marginalization, especially of those whose Patterns do not fit the Pattern bias of educational institutions.
- LML in its completeness is a form of reflective practice; it makes central the comparison of intentions to actions and their outcomes through its metacognitive emphasis and tools; it generates

data useful for assessing congruence/incongruence; its shared theory and lexicon support individual and shared critical reflective thought and data analysis.

- LML promotes learner-focused teaching by providing teachers with the ultimate reward: seeing their students learn.

> LML promotes learner-focused teaching by providing teachers with the ultimate reward: seeing their students learn.

- LML, when used with fidelity, enhances learning, engagement, competence, autonomy, relatedness, trust, transparency, caring, respect, listening, coaching, feedback, group process and function, shared decision making, problem finding/framing, problem solving, multidimensional knowledge, and appreciation of people. It reduces power differentials, interpersonal conflicts, and student marginalization.
- LML at the "deeply embedded" phase of development is completely integrated with curriculum and teaching of content; it simply enhances the learning of the intended curriculum.
- LML, through personal knowledge of self as learner and learning strategy development, empowers students to do well on all types of assessments and enhances their performance on state and district learning standards.
- LML recognizes three Mental Processes; (1) Affectation and (2) Conation are equal partners with (3) Cognition; thus, LML addresses the wholeness of human functioning and learning.
- LML differs from all styles-based concepts and products grounded in personality theory, which go only as far as describing and classifying individuals and make teachers responsible for altering the environment to fit the learner. Only LML provides a theory of brain-mind connection, a lexicon accessible to all ages that makes possible discussion of learning in real time, and a metacognitive thrust with tools to support it that enables a learner to alter the learning context by assessing learning tasks and creating strategies for temporarily changing one's natural Pattern dominance for enhanced task performance.

12

Epilogue

Honoring Intentional Teaching

Laurie's Gift

Laurie (S28 P23 T22 C17) arrives at the door, a large shopping bag in hand. "I have your present," she announces cheerily setting her bag down on a chair. She reaches inside.

"This reminded me of your Confluence," she says, removing a bonsai cherry tree from the bag and handing it to me. It is truly a work of living art, a wondrous thing: a flurry of tiny emerald leaves on top with beautifully intertwining roots and miniature branches below. Balanced and calm at the center, it is perfectly trimmed in some places and a wild jumble in others. It is just so cool to imagine how it had been shaped over time. I'll have to learn more about how to care for it, I think.

We admire the little stones placed around the base of the planter, the moss, and all the intricacies of the tree's design as we stand there. Laurie is beaming. I probably am, too. I am so taken aback by the unexpectedness of this gesture.

Laurie sees me, I think, as we continue to examine the bonsai tree, admiring it from all angles. This is completely me.

In that moment, she realizes something. "Your thank you card!" she says and begins rummaging through the bag, to no avail.

"I don't know where your card is," she says after a moment. "I can't find it." She suddenly looks at once rueful and apologetic.

"No matter. You and I both know what we want to say. And this little tree says it best, don't you think?" She nods, hugs me, and without ceremony, continues along her way to distribute her other last-day-of-school gifts.

> *As I stand in my near-empty classroom, surrounded by stacks of numbered textbooks and piles of graded projects still to be returned, I examine the little bonsai again and smile to myself. As a learner who is Use First in Sequence and Avoid in Confluence, Laurie recognizes and values the Pattern in me that I value most in myself—Confluence. I feel incredibly honored to receive such clear validation of one learner's understanding of me.*

Bonnie's Reflection

Most gifts I receive from students and their families I send forth in the world to enjoy a second life beyond me. After having taught for so long, there's a limit to how many notepads I can use, how much hand soap I can consume, though in the moment, I always appreciate the sentiment behind the kind gesture.

I did keep the tiny tree, however, because it reminded me that I made a difference in the life of that learner. She saw my intentions and accepted the imperfections I have. I will never be a perfect teacher; teaching is an art and a daily practice. But I am engaged in the mindful tending of my work, in the lifelong pursuit of becoming the teacher I still aspire to be. The Let Me Learn Process, embedded in me now, has enabled me to do intentional pruning of my teaching.

> The Let Me Learn Process, embedded in me now, has enabled me to do intentional pruning of my teaching.

I can say with assurance that many adults I've worked with don't know me as a learner, as Laurie did, despite the hours we've logged as professionals sharing the same workspace. In seeking to unmask the mystery of schooling, I made myself transparent to the students in every way I knew how: I disclosed to them how I learn, and how they can come to understand how they learn. I gave them a new way to think about getting along with others and strategies to use so that they could experience success and become more independent learners.

I made my learning public and let students into my thinking so that they could understand how I operate in the schooling system as a fellow learner. I sought to reduce the power differential separating learners from teachers as authority figures. I made it clear that some learners would be harder for me to know and to teach because of my Patterns and that I would need their help. I would persevere to find solutions to their learning until I found a match between us that worked.

I acknowledged to my learners when I was too controlling, too independent, or too talkative because of my combination of Learning Patterns. I shared with them the challenges of Forging an extreme Avoid in Technical Reasoning, which makes me quick to dismiss my ability to problem solve, therefore, frequently short-circuiting my learning. I learned to ask for more help from others, to mean it and to take feedback and utilize it.

Laurie's symbolic gift confirmed that she understood what it was that I was trying each day to offer her: a greater understanding, ultimately, of how all learners must engage in mindful, intentional scrutiny to understand what makes them unique so that they can use this powerful knowledge to learn, change, and grow. All are inter-twined. I will never forget how grateful I was for that very powerful gesture of honoring me as an intentional teacher of learners.

Appendix

Additional Information About the Let Me Learn Process

Understanding the Learning Pattern Scores

The first section of the Appendix is a more detailed portrayal of the section Understanding How Our Patterns Affect Our Learning in Chapter 1 (pages 11–13). The following figures provide more information for understanding how a Use First level of each of the four Patterns plays itself out in our thoughts, actions, feelings, and internal chatter. In addition, there are figures indicating how the opposite end of the Learning Connections Inventory (LCI) scores, the Avoid level, plays itself out in each of the four Patterns. Thus, you have the two poles of the LCI score continuum to consult. The Use As Needed level lies between the two extremes; it has a positive presentation but is less forceful than the depiction in the Use First level figures. These richer descriptions should enable you to grasp a better understanding of how your LCI scores manifest themselves in pursuing learning tasks.

Sequence

If your scale score for Sequence is between 25 and 35, you use Sequence at a Use First level. That indicates you want the following:

- Clear directions
- Step-by-step directions
- Time to do work neatly (see Figure A.1 for more detail)

Figure A.1 If You Use Sequence First

How You Think	How You Do Things	How You Feel	Your Internal Self-Talk Sometimes Said Aloud
I think in steps seeking to follow each aspect of the directions.	I break tasks down into steps.	I feel confident when I have clear directions.	Could we review those directions one more time, just to make sure?
I think in categories.	I list and organize.	I feel relieved when the system I organized works.	There is a place for everything and everything is in its place.
I have a plan in mind.	I work the plan!	I am frustrated when the plan changes.	Don't keep changing the plan and the directions!

However, if your scale score for Sequence is 17 to 7, you Avoid Sequence. That indicates you do not do the following:

- Value directions
- Plan or live by a schedule
- Double-check your work
- Follow directions easily (see Figure A.2 for more detail)

Figure A.2 If You Avoid Sequence

How You Think	How You Do Things	How You Feel	Your Internal Self-Talk Sometimes Said Aloud
These directions make no sense!	I don't read the directions.	I feel confused by the wording and the order of the directions.	Why do I have to follow directions?
I did this before. Why repeat it?	I don't practice and rehearse.	I feel bored when forced to practice and rehearse.	Do I have to do it again?
Why can't I just jump in?	I fail to do all of the parts of the task leaving some incomplete.	I feel not bound by the rules or the requirements of the task.	Does it matter what I do first? Can't I just start wherever I want? Why all the fuss?

Precision

If your scale score for Precision is between 25 and 35, you use Precision at a Use First level. That indicates you want to do the following:

- Receive thorough explanations
- Ask many questions
- Answer questions
- Be accurate and correct
- Analyze test results
- Have written documentation (see Figure A.3 for more detail)

Figure A.3   If You Use Precision First

How You Think	How You Do Things	How You Feel	Your Internal Self-Talk Sometimes Said Aloud
I think in information.	I write things down and document everything.	I feel confident when I have my notes or journal to refer to.	Before I decide, I need more information.
I think knowing facts means I am smart.	I leave no piece of information unspoken.	I hate being "out of the know."	Well actually did you know that . . .
I think knowledge is power.	I research information and check sources.	I feel frustrated when incorrect information is accepted as valid.	Where did you get that information?

If your scale score for Precision is 17 to 7, you Avoid it. That indicates you do the following:

- Rarely read for pleasure
- Don't attend to details
- Find memorizing tedious
- Hear wordy conversation as "blah, blah, blah" (see Figure A.4 for more detail)

Figure A.4 If You Avoid Precision

How You Think	How You Do Things	How You Feel	Your Internal Self-Talk Sometimes Said Aloud
How am I supposed to know all this stuff?	I don't have specific answers.	I become angry at not having the one right answer.	Don't expect me to know names and dates!
What are these pages and pages of stuff?	I skim instead of read details.	Pages of words make my head hurt.	Do I have to read all of this? Is there a DVD I can watch instead?
What information is important and what am I expected to write down?	I take few, if any, notes.	I am fearful of looking stupid because my notes are so few.	Why write this down? I can use Google if I really want to find information.

Technical Reasoning

If your scale score for Technical Reasoning is between 25 and 35, you use Technical Reasoning at a Use First level. This indicates you do the following:

- Look for relevance and practicality
- Don't use many words
- Believe you can fix things
- Prefer to work by yourself (see Figure A.5 for more detail)

Figure A.5 If You Use Technical Reasoning First

How You Think	How You Do Things	How You Feel	Your Internal Self-Talk Sometimes Said Aloud
What value does this have in the real world?	I attack real or virtual problems.	I feel frustrated when the task has no real world relevance.	Why do I need to know or do this?
I figure out how something works without using words.	I work in my head and then with my hands.	I enjoy competing with myself when figuring out how something works.	This is the challenge I've been looking for. Stand back and give me some space to get started.

How You Think	How You Do Things	How You Feel	Your Internal Self-Talk Sometimes Said Aloud
I don't want to read a book about it; I want to get my hands on it.	I tinker.	I like the feel of having the right tool or instrument in my hand to get the job done.	I can't wait to get my hands on this!

If your scale score for Technical Reasoning is 17 to 7, you Avoid it. This indicates you do the following:

- Hire others to do building and repair work
- Don't venture into the tool aisle
- Problem solve with others, not alone
- Find it difficult to understand why some people use few words to express themselves (see Figure A.6 for more detail)

Figure A.6 If You Avoid Technical Reasoning

How You Think	How You Do Things	How You Feel	Your Internal Self-Talk Sometimes Said Aloud
Why should I care how this works?	I Avoid fixing or repairing things.	I am inept.	I don't care how it runs; I just want it to run!
Somebody has to help me figure this out!	I talk about it instead of doing it.	I feel frustrated because I can't conceptualize the functions involved in solving the issue.	I'm an educated person; I should be able to solve this!
Why do I have to make something?	I rely on reading the directions or finding an example to follow to assemble or build a project.	I am very comfortable with my words and thoughts—not tools.	Why can't I just talk or write about it?

Confluence

If your score for Confluence is between 25 and 35, you use Confluence at a Use First level. That indicates that you do the following:

- Thrive on generating new ideas
- Use imagination to a high degree
- Seek risk-taking opportunities
- Do not fear failure but see it as an opportunity to learn and grow (see Figure A.7 for more detail)

Figure A.7   If You Use Confluence First

How You Think	How You Do Things	How You Feel	Your Internal Self-Talk Sometimes Said Aloud
Why not take a chance—what can I lose?	I take risks.	I am not afraid to risk failure.	I can always start over and learn from my mistakes.
I think of new ways to do conventional approaches.	I brainstorm and improvise.	I enjoy testing the boundaries.	I have an idea. I have another idea!
I connect things in my mind that are seemingly unrelated.	I read between the lines and intuit meaning.	I am energized by making connections that others don't see.	Don't you see the connection? It's so clear to me.

If your scale score for Confluence is 17 to 7, you Avoid it. This indicates you do the following:

- Think taking risks is foolish and wasteful
- Would rather *not* make mistakes
- Are cautious in how you go about making life decisions (see Figure A.8 for more detail)

| Figure A.8 | If You Avoid Confluence |

How You Think	How You Do Things	How You Feel	Your Internal Self-Talk Sometimes Said Aloud
Has this been well thought out?	I don't start anything new without a plan.	I feel unsettled.	Let's not lose sight of the plan. Stay focused!
I hate brainstorming!	I Avoid improvising at the last minute.	I feel left out because I can't come up with ideas fast enough.	Where did that idea come from?
What do you mean, *imagine*?	I can't follow "outside of the box" thinking.	This is out of control!	Get a grip! Let's deal with current realities not fantasies!

Patterns in the Use As Needed Range

If any of your Patterns are in the 18 to 24 range, then they are Use As Needed. You can use them when you need to. You just don't feel a great urgency to do so, especially if they fall into the 18 to 21 range. These Patterns tend to lay dormant until you need to wake them up and let them know that you need to use them *now*!

Decoding a Learning Task

Once you have a good grasp of how your LCI scores translate into your thoughts, actions, feelings, and internal chatter, the next step is Decoding, which requires that you determine the degree to which each Pattern must be used in order to complete a given task effectively.

The Skill of Decoding

Using the examples that follow, examine how Decoding works. First, read the guidelines or directions for the task. Circle the key words that are intended to direct your action. Label each according to the Pattern it is directing you to use. Finally, analyze the amount of time you need to invest in using each of your Patterns to complete the task successfully. Say, for example, the task is to, "Write in bulleted form a brief description of your newly installed security system." Your Patterns are Sequence 28, Precision 17, Technical Reasoning 26, and Confluence 21. Without Decoding this task in its entirety, you may shut down because your Avoid Precision 17 does not appreciate the word, "write." In fact, writing is something you just don't want to do. However, if you allow your Avoidance of Precision to keep you from reading the rest of the task description, you will fail when, in fact, you could have succeeded by using your Technical Reasoning and Sequential Patterns to overcome the frustration of Avoiding Precision. Other examples of Decoding appear in Figure A.9. Examine their wording and Decoding.

Figure A.9   Examples of Decoded Instructions

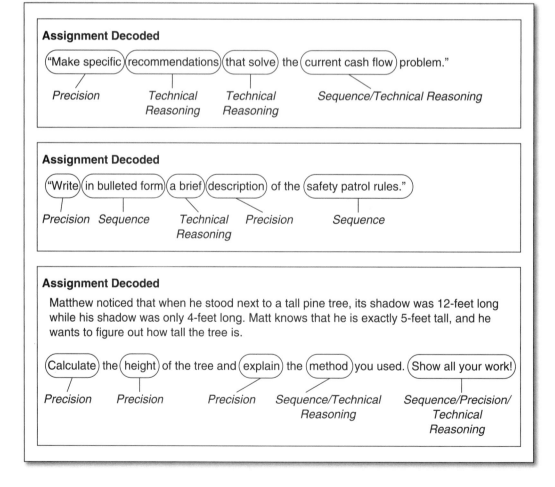

Clearly, Decoding tasks makes them understandable and doable. Students enjoy breaking the code of assignments because they know that by doing so they will tackle the task with greater success and less frustration and wasted energy. Decoding your assignments as you make your instructional plans will also provide you with an insight into what Patterns you require students to use the most and whether there is an equal distribution of required Pattern usage in your classroom.

The Skill of Listening to the Internal Talk of Your Patterns: Metacognating

In the previous pages, you have read that Let Me Learn (LML) "is an Advanced Learning System that prepares all learners to be accountable for their learning outcomes." The explanation that follows demonstrates how that claim is achieved. The process used by learners to control their four Learning Patterns while engaged in a learning task is called the Metacognitive Process.

Metacognition in the LML lexicon is defined as our internal chatter or talk—the voices of our Patterns talking, arguing, and negotiating how to proceed and how to achieve—how to reach our learning goals. A broad description of internal or self-talk, including Pattern associated talk, has already been presented indirectly in the details of Figures A.1 through A.8. The kind of talk in these figures goes on in learners all the time, but it is often unrecognized. LML helps learners tune in directly to this chatter within them and formulate strategies to use their Patterns with intention.

The LML Metacognitive Process consists of a series of phases through which learners move as they seek to make sense of and respond to a specific learning task. LML uses seven verbs to describe the Metacognitive Process: (1) Mull, (2) Connect, (3) Rehearse, (4) Express, (5) Assess, (6) Reflect, and (7) Revisit. Use of these terms fosters real-time double-loop learning. The seven phases of talk are described below. Teachers often demonstrate the phases using what is called the Metacognitive Drill, a step-by-step practice of the Metacognitive Process. The phases of the Drill are depicted in Figure A.10 and described here:

- Mull is considering, even wallowing in, the description or directions of an assignment until the learner understands the task expectations and how to make a conscious effort to begin his or her learning. Mulling may take minutes, hours, even days depending on the nature of the task and the Patterns of the learner.

- Connect involves relating the current learning context to prior learning experiences, gathering and reading information, asking questions, and reviewing previous learning. It may include linking up with a peer who can model what needs to be done and how to do it.

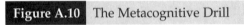

Figure A.10 The Metacognitive Drill

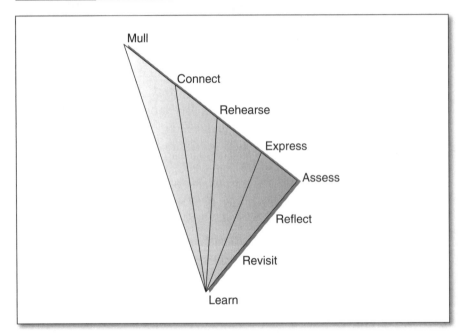

- Rehearse is exactly that—it is done privately and the only audience (and critic) is the learner—him or herself.
- Express is the public performance of knowledge and/or a specific skill, which opens the individual to receiving public feedback.
- Assess is the student's means of weighing his or her performance against the expectations for a specific task. Think of the scale of justice. Then ask, "Did my performance balance with the requirements of the task?"
- Reflect is viewing a handheld mirror, facing oneself, and asking, "What specifically did I do or not do that resulted in this learning outcome?" This is the heart of becoming an intentional learner, the phase where the buck stops.

- Revisit is returning to the original learning task, a similar task, or an extension of that task and applying what was learned through the phases of Assess and Reflect for an earlier task. This phase fosters measureable improvement based on implementing new learning strategies.

Arguably, the most underused phases are Assess, Reflect, and Revisit because these are seldom, if ever, part of experience in school or work. The LML Process seeks to reverse that neglect by encouraging and reinforcing the learner's use of strategies by providing a safe, nonpunitive environment in which to reconsider strategies that worked or did not work.

Teachers who are aware of the Metacognitive Process and the chatter occurring in the learners within the classroom will often use the vocabulary that comprises the Metacognitive Drill to check on how students are progressing. For example, how many are still Mulling 10 minutes into an assignment? How many have Connected and moved on to quiet Rehearsal? Who has skipped these processes and moved on to Express or even Assess?

Knowing how various learners are responding to a given assignment and having the terms to explain progress or lack thereof in nonpejorative terms can enhance both the learning environment and the teacher's ability to respond and intervene appropriately.

Glossary of Let Me Learn Terms

Advanced Learning System refers to Let Me Learn's (LML) system for developing intentional learners. The system includes a specific learning theory (the Interactive Learning Model); learning tools (the Learning Connections Inventory [LCI], the Learner Profile, the Metacognitive Drill, and the Strategy Card); an array of skills (Decoding, metacognating, and FITing), and a specific learning lexicon of terms that make up the LML Process.

Affectation refers to our feelings of worth and value as learners. This Mental Process focuses our emotive response to a learning task.

Assess refers to an individual's means of weighing his or her performance against another's expectations for a specific task. This phase within an individual's metacognitive cycle launches reflective practice.

Avoid Pattern refers to Learning Connections Inventory (LCI) scale scores that range from 7 to 17. An Avoid has a Pattern volume equal to a Use First Pattern. It will make itself heard in a learner's internal metacognitive chatter. When an individual Avoids a Pattern, he or she will feel stress whenever asked to use that Pattern without the benefit of intentional strategies.

Bridge Learner refers to a learner whose Learning Connections Inventory (LCI) scores fall between 18 to 24 in all four Patterns and can apply each Pattern on Use As Needed basis. "I learn from listening to others and interacting with them. I am comfortable using all of the Patterns. Sometimes I feel like a jack-of-all-trades and a master of none, but I also find I can blend in, pitch in, and help make things happen as a contributing member of the group. I weigh things in the balance before I act. I lead from the middle by encouraging others rather than taking charge of a situation."

Cognition refers to our internal processing of information. This Mental Process focuses on thinking.

Conation refers to the pace, skill, autonomy, and manner with which we perform a task. This Mental Process focuses on the *doing* of a learning task.

Confluence refers to the Pattern that describes the way we use our imagination, take initiative and risks, and brainstorm ways of approaching things in a unique manner. Confluence allows the learner to link disparate pieces of information into the big picture.

Connect refers to relating the current learning context to prior learning experiences, gathering and reading information, asking questions, and reviewing previous learning. It may also mean linking up with a peer in the classroom who can model what needs to be done and how to do it. This phase within an individual's metacognitive cycle launches Reflection on previous learning.

Curiosity and intrigue refers to the first stage of immersion into the Let Me Learn (LML) Process. At this level, the process looks interesting and worthy of attention.

Decoding refers to analyzing a task to determine the degree to which each of the four Patterns is required to complete the task successfully. Used as a way for learners to Assess how to apply their Patterns (i.e., Tether, Intensify, or Forge their use).

Deeply embedded refers to the sixth and deepest level of immersion into the Let Me Learn (LML) Process. At this level, we can't think about learning or teaching without using the concepts and constructs of the LML Process because they now form the bedrock of our learning and teaching self.

Dynamic Learner refers to a learner who has a set of Learning Connections Inventory (LCI) scale scores that use one or two Patterns at the Use First level and any other combination of Avoid or Use As Needed for the remaining Patterns. The combination of Use First with the other Use As Needed or Avoid Patterns creates a dynamic different than either a Bridge Learner (one whose all four scale scores lie between 18–24) or a Strong-willed Learner (one who uses three or more Use First Patterns resulting in the learner's sense of being his or her own team).

Express refers to the public performance of knowledge and/or a specific skill. This phase within an individual's metacognitive cycle typically follows rehearsing. Publicly performing the task opens the individual to receiving public feedback.

Forge refers to increasing the use of an individual's Avoid level of a specific Learning Pattern for that person to succeed in completing a specific task. An individual can Forge his or her use of a Pattern by as much as five points for a limited time. Forging requires intention, strategies, and focused energy.

Group Covenant refers to a written agreement among members of a team to work as a cooperative unit to achieve a specific goal. Implicit in the Covenant agreement is the willingness to honor one another's Learning Patterns and resolve Pattern conflicts as they arise. Most important, the Covenant includes how its members will support and mentor one another in the use of their Patterns.

Insights and understandings refers to the fifth stage of immersion into the Let Me Learn (LML) Process. At this level, we gain perspectives beyond the superficial levels and begin to address issues at the heart of learning and teaching.

Intensify refers to increasing the use of an individual's Use As Needed Pattern to a more forceful volume or level. An individual can Intensify his or her use of a Pattern by as much as five points for a limited time. Intensifying requires intention, strategies, and focused energy.

Intentional Learning refers to making the learning experience work for the individual by Decoding the task, matching the Pattern use required to the individual's Patterns, and then strategizing how to Forge, Intensify, or Tether the individual's Patterns to meet those of the task.

Intentional Teaching refers to the teacher's knowledge of his or her Learning Processes and how they shape the learning environment and activities the teacher brings to the classroom. Next, Intentional Teaching involves a conscious effort on the part of the teacher to respect, value, and mentor the personal Learning Processes of his or her students. Finally, Intentional Teaching relies on communicating with students about their Learning Processes vis-a-vis their peers and their teacher. Intentional Teaching creates a dialogue about learning inside and outside the classroom.

Interactive Learning Model (ILM) refers to the simultaneous interactions of three Mental Processes, identified as Cognition, Conation, and Affectation, which operate concurrently within each of the four operational Patterns that make up each learner's brain-mind interface. The model developed by Christine Johnston (1994) is based on research conducted in cognitive psychology, learning theory, multiple intelligences, and neuroscience.

Internal chatter see Metacognition and Metacognitive Process

Interpreting Learning Connections Inventory Scores refers to interpreting the scale scores of an individual for each of the four Learning Patterns. Because of the interpretation, an individual can anticipate how he or she will respond to a particular task based on his or her Patterns.

Learning refers to our ability to take in the world around us and make sense of it so that we can respond to it in an efficient, effective, and appropriate manner.

Learning Connections Inventory (LCI) refers to the instrument, a two-part 28-question self-report tool with three open-response written questions. It is administered to identify an individual's combination of Learning Patterns. Responses to the 28 items are tallied forming a score representing the degree to which an individual uses each of four Learning Patterns: Sequence, Precision, Technical Reasoning, and Confluence. Each score is placed on a continuum that indicates the range or of level of use of each Pattern: Use First, Use As Needed, and Avoid.

Learning Connections Inventory (LCI) charts refers to a visual tool used to present LCI scores of individuals, showing each of their four Patterns, typically expressed in the following order: Sequence, Precision, Technical Reasoning, and Confluence.

Learning Patterns/Learning Processes (used interchangeably) refer to Sequence, Precision, Technical Reasoning, and Confluence. Within each of these Patterns, the source and degree of the Cognitive, Conation, and Affective characteristics of each determine the level to which an individual naturally uses each.

Let Me Learn (LML) community refers to those individuals and organizations presently using the LML Process with intention.

Let Me Learn (LML) integrated system see Advanced Learning System

Let Me Learn (LML) Process refers to an Advanced Learning System whose intellectual property and logo are registered as a trademark with the U.S. Patent Office.

Mental Processes refer to the Cognition, Conation, and Affectation occurring within each discrete Learning Pattern.

Metacognition in its traditional use refers to thinking about one's thinking. The term means much more when used within the context of the Let Me Learn (LML) Process. Metacognition as an LML term refers to the ability to hear the talk (sometimes referred to an internal chatter) among one's Learning Patterns and respond to the talk by using personal strategies to intervene in negative talk and respond positively to use one's Learning Processes with intention.

Metacognitive Drill refers to the seven terms Let Me Learn (LML) uses to explain what the learner is experiencing as he or she is completing a learning task. These terms include Mull, Connect, Rehearse, Express, Assess, Reflect, and Revisit.

Metacognitive Process refers to the phases of internal talk (internal chatter) that occur among an individual's four Patterns as he or she considers the task before him or her.

Mull refers to considering, contemplating, even wallowing in the description or directions of an assignment until the learner is able to understand the expectations of the task and how he or she can make a conscious effort to begin his or her learning. Mulling may take minutes, hours, or even days depending on the nature of the task to be accomplished and the Patterns of the learner seeking to respond to the task.

Niggling concern refers to the third stage of immersion into the Let Me Learn (LML) Process. At this level, we are confronted with a significant problem that arises for which we want a solution. At this level, now we remember—perhaps—that LML stuff could actually help.

Pain and growth refers to the fourth stage of immersion into the Let Me Learn (LML) Process. At this level, we begin to experience some pain and awkwardness because we are beginning to use metacognitive tools to solve significant challenges. This is a stage marked by significant personal growth in using the LML Process. Serious use of reflective practice and double-loop learning begins at this deeper level.

Patterns see Learning Patterns/Learning Processes

Pattern bias is usually associated with assumptions about Use First and Avoid Patterns and refers to the assumption or the belief that a specific Pattern combination is not as desirable as another. The root of Pattern bias is frequently an unintentional preference for one's own use of Learning Patterns. Pattern bias affects an individual's appreciation for and acceptance of another's approach to completing a task or producing work product.

Pattern characteristics refers to the results of factor analyzing the responses of more than 5,000 six- to eighteen-year-olds and 4,000 adults who responded to the various iterations of the Learning Connections Inventory during its development. Those factors that clustered together were then given a categorical label. The labels chosen were the following: Sequence, Precision, Technical Reasoning, and Confluence.

Pattern combination refers to any combination of an individual's four Learning Patterns.

Pattern conflict refers to the negative interaction of individuals because of pronounced Pattern differences; the conflict is generated because of individuals' lack of intentional communication concerning their differences in how each approaches learning.

Pattern difference refers to the difference of Pattern combinations between/among individuals.

Pattern driven refers to an activity that becomes overwhelmingly associated with the use of one Pattern not a balance of four Patterns used in consort.

Pattern FIT refers to the appropriate use of Patterns to undertake a task successfully, the match between the task to be done and the Pattern levels available to do the job.

Pattern validity refers to processes that examine whether Learning Connections Inventory (LCI) scores authentically represent the way a learner uses his or her Patterns in combination. The first step to establishing Pattern validity is to match Pattern scale scores to what the person has written as his or her short-answer responses. This process known as "validating the LCI scores" uses a protocol for identifying words reflective of specific Patterns. This internal LCI validity check helps strengthen reliance that an individual's Learning Profile (LCI) is accurate for that individual (See C. Johnston & Dainton, 2004).

Pattern volume refers to equating a Pattern's use with a voice volume to demonstrate the degree to which a Pattern's attributes influence the learner's behavior. Use First Patterns are equated to being playground volumes, Use As Needed as classroom volumes, and Avoid usage are soft-spoken or whisper volumes. Individuals learn to adjust the volume to match the Pattern combination to the task at hand through metacognitive awareness and intention.

Personal Learning Profile refers to a record of your Learning Patterns described in one's own words. It is a way of translating the Pattern scores into an authentic Profile of one's self as a learner.

Phases of development in the Let Me Learn (LML) Process refers to six phases cited with the following terms: curiosity and intrigue, play and stay, niggling concern, pain and growth, insights and understanding, deeply embedded.

Play and stay refers to the second stage of immersion into the Let Me Learn (LML) Process. At this level, we are using the process but we're staying at a superficial level of involvement (we know the Patterns; we use the words). We're comfortable enough to remain here. Moving on to metacognition is too much work and doesn't seem necessary yet.

Precision refers to the Learning Pattern that seeks information and details, asks and answers questions, researches and documents facts, and critically examines information for any flaws.

Range see Learning Connections Inventory (LCI)

Reflect refers to looking in a mirror, facing oneself, and asking, "What specifically did I or did I not do that resulted in this learning outcome?" Reflection is an inward directed activity that reinforces the ownership of the individual's learning strategies and intentional behaviors. This metacognitive phase follows Assessment. This is the heart of becoming an intentional learner. This is where the buck stops.

Rehearse refers to privately practicing a response to a learning task. The only audience (and critic) is the learner himself or herself.

Revisit refers to revisiting the original learning task, a similar task, or an extension of that task (new assignment) and applying what was learned through the metacognitive phases of Assess and Reflect. This is where transferrable skills are applied to a specific task with the intention of demonstrating improvement over the previous performance. This metacognitive phase fosters measureable improvement based on the implementation of new learning strategies.

School Patterns refers to Patterns that are frequently but unintentionally honored in school and/or classroom settings because of the bias of teachers for their Patterns. Elementary and middle School Patterns honored are usually Sequence and Precision because the overwhelming majority of these teachers lead with Sequence and Precision themselves.

Score see Learning Connections Inventory (LCI)

Sequence refers to the Learning Pattern that needs to organize, plan, and complete work assignments without interruption using clear instructions as well as a time frame that allows for checking work.

Strategy Card refers to a charted representation of the gap between a learner's Patterns and a particular task to be completed. A strategy of specific actions is written by the learner for those Patterns that the learner recognizes need to be Tethered, Forged, or Intensified to undertake the task successfully.

Strong-willed Learner refers to learners whose scores are 25 or more in at least three out of four Patterns. "I am my own team. I prefer to work alone so that I can control the plan, the ideas, the talk, the decisions, the process, and the outcomes. I lead from out in front. Sometimes others find it hard to follow my lead."

Team of Patterns see Pattern combination

Technical Reasoning refers to the Pattern that describes the way we seek relevant real-world experiences and practical answers. This is the Pattern of the fewest words. It emphasizes the ability to problem solve using independent, private thinking and hands-on interaction.

Tether refers to restraining the use of a Use First Learning Pattern. This is done with intention to allow the learner's other Patterns to be heard metacognitively and to operate more effectively.

Use As Needed refers to Learning Connections Inventory (LCI) scale scores that range from 18 to 24. These Patterns tend to be lost among the more vocal Pattern chatter of Use First and Avoid Patterns.

Use First refers to Learning Connections Inventory (LCI) scale scores that range from 25 to 35. A Use First Pattern has a volume equal to an Avoid Pattern. It will make itself heard in a learner's internal metacognitive chatter. Learners use this Pattern first and begin their learning task relying on it.

Word Wall refers to posters or charts that list words associated with each of the four Patterns: Sequence, Precision, Technical Reasoning, and Confluence. The posters provide learners with assistance in doing task analysis and creating Strategy Cards. (These are available from www.letmelearn.org/store.)

Working memory refers to the memory function that receives stimuli that have passed through the interface of our Learning Patterns and now require translation into symbolic representation (words, numbers, musical notes, and the like) as well as intentional storage for ready retrieval.

References

Addy, L. (1996, April). *Challenging the assumptions: The motivation and learning of children who have developmental coordination disorder.* Paper presented at the annual meeting of the American Educational Research Association, New York.

Borg, M. (1996, April). *A factor analysis of primary school student responses: The test of a learning instrument's validity.* Paper presented at the annual meeting of the American Educational Research Association, New York.

Borg, C. & Calleja, C. (2006). Using technical and confluent patterns first: A recipe for underachievement? In C. Borg & C. Calleja, (Eds.), *Understanding children and youth at risk: Narratives of hope* (pp. 127–151). Blata 1-Bajda, Malta: Agenda.

Bruer, J. (1994). *Schools for thought.* Cambridge, MA: MIT Press.

Buchanan, P. (2005, November). *Leadership and learning.* Annual conference of the Society of Women Engineers, Los Angeles, CA.

Calleja, C. (1998). *Listening to the learner: Learner's characteristics to shape whole school reform* (Unpublished master's thesis). Faculty of Education, University of Malta, Msida, Malta.

Campbell, N. (2005, November). *Putting learning to work.* Annual conference of the Society of Women Engineers, Los Angeles, CA.

Curry, L. (1990). A critique of the research on learning styles. *Educational Leadership, 48*(2), 50–56.

Dawkins, B. U. (2008). *Honoring the learner: One teacher's experience implementing the Let Me Learn Process* (Unpublished doctoral dissertation). Hofstra University, Hempstead, NY.

Dien, J., Franklin, M. S., Michelson, C. A., Lemen, L. C., Adams, C. L., & Kiehl, K. A. (2008). fMRI characterization of the language formulation area. *Brain Research, 1229*(10), 179–192.

Freese, S. F. (1999). *The relationship between teacher caring and student engagement in academic high school classes.* (Unpublished doctoral dissertation). Hofstra University, Hempstead, NY.

Gardner, H. (1983). *Frames of mind: The theory of multiple intelligences.* New York: Basic Books.

Hayes, M. (1996, April). *Finding the voice: Hearing the voice—The under-represented in the reform movement.* Paper presented at the annual meeting of the American Educational Research Association, New York.

Heredia, A. (1999). *Cultural learning styles.* ERIC Clearinghouse on Teaching and Teacher Education. (Eric Digest Number: 1999–10)

Irvine, J., & York, D. (1995). Learning styles and culturally diverse students: A literature review. In J. A. Banks & C. A. M. Banks (Eds.), *Handbook of research on cultural education* (pp. 484–497). New York: Macmillan.

Johnston, C. (1994). *Unlocking the will to learn.* Paper presented at the twentieth annual meeting of the British Educational Research Association, Queen Anne's College, Oxford, UK.

Johnston, C. (1996). *Let Me Learn.* Thousand Oaks, CA: Corwin.

Johnston, C. (2000). *A personal guide to implementing the LML Process K–12.* Pittsgrove, NJ: Learning Connections Resources.

Johnston, C. (2003). *Drop dead data.* Keynote presentation at the seventh annual Let Me Learn Summer Institute, Philadelphia.

Johnston, C. (2005, September). *Communicating from the inside out.* Keynote presentation at the National Writing Conference, Tumas Dingli School, Hal Warda Street, Attard, Malta.

Johnston, C. (2006). *Promoting mindful learning in the mindless school.* Keynote presentation at the Let Me Learn International Conference, Sunshine Coast University, Queensland, Australia.

Johnston, C. (2007). *Finding your way: Navigating life by understanding your learning self.* Unpublished manuscript.

Johnston, C., & Dainton, G. (1997). *The learning combinations inventory manual.* Turnersville, NJ: Learning Connections Resources.

Johnston, C., & Dainton, G. (2004). *The learning connections inventory manual* (2nd ed.). Turnersville, NJ: Learning Connections Resources.

Johnston, J. (1996, April). *Many voices—One message: A cross-cultural study of student learning processes with implications for learners, teachers and reformers . . . will the real learner raise a hand?* Paper presented at the annual meeting of the American Educational Research Association, New York.

Kottkamp, R. B. (2002). *The problematic student.* Poster session presented at the fifth annual Let Me Learn Summer Institute, Philadelphia.

Kottkamp, R. B. (2006). *Unrecognized bias in high-stakes writing tests.* Presentation at the ninth annual Let Me Learn Summer Institute, Vineland, NJ.

Kottkamp, R. B., & Rusch, E. A. (2009). The landscape of scholarship on the education of school leaders, 1985–2006. In M. D. Young, G. M. Crow, J. Murphy, & R. T. Ogawa (Eds.), *Handbook of research on the education of school leaders* (pp. 23–84). New York: Routledge, Taylor and Francis.

Kottkamp, R. B., & Silverberg, R. P. (1999). *Exploring the mental models of administrative aspirants: Assumptions about students, teaching and learning.* Paper presented at the annual meeting of the American Educational Research Association, Montreal, Canada.

Kottkamp, R. B., & Silverberg, R. P. (2006). Reconceptualizing students at risk: Teacher assumptions about "the problematic student." In C. Borg & C. Calleja (Eds.), *Understanding children and youth at risk: Narratives of hope* (pp. 31–63). Blata 1- Bajda, Malta: Agenda.

Lortie, D. C. (1975). *Schoolteacher: A sociological study.* Chicago: University of Chicago Press.

Lowry, L. (1993). *The giver.* Boston: Houghton Mifflin.

Marcellino, P. A. (2001). *Learning to be a team: A case study of action research in a graduate business management course.* (Unpublished doctoral dissertation). Hofstra University, Hempstead, NY.

McCrone, J. (2000). 'Right brain' or 'left brain'—Myth or reality? [Electronic version] *The New Scientist.* Retrieved March 24, 2010, from http://www.rbiproduction.co.uk

McSweeney, R. T. (2005). *Merging cognitive and instructional theories into instructional practice in secondary mathematics: The impact of an advanced learning system implementation on teacher beliefs, student affect and achievement* (Unpublished doctoral dissertation). Hofstra University, Hempstead, NY.

Mifsud, J. (1996, April). *Listening to the learner: Harnessing learner characteristics to shape school reform.* Paper presented at the annual meeting of the American Educational Research Association, New York.

Myers Briggs, I., Mcaulley, M. H., Quenk, N. L., & Hammer, A. (1998). *MBTI manual: A guide to the development and use of the Myers Briggs type indicator* (3rd ed.). Paolo Alto, CA: Consulting Psychologists Press.

New York State Education Department. (2009). *English language arts: Standard 3.* Retrieved March 24, 2010, from http://www.emsc.nysed.gov/ciai/ela/elastandards/elamap.html

Osterman, K. F. (1994). Feedback in school settings: No news is bad news. *Journal of Management Science, 6*(4), 28–44.

Osterman, K. F. (2000). Students' need for belonging in the school community. *Review of Educational Research, 70*(3), 323–367.

Osterman, K. F., & Kottkamp, R. B. (2004). *Reflective practice for educators: Improving student learning* (2nd ed.). Newbury Park, CA: Corwin.

Paulsen, G. (1998). *My life in dog years.* New York: Random House.

Silverberg, R. P. (2002). *From marginalization to relational space: A descriptive phenomenological study of teachers who changed their assumptions and beliefs about problematic students* (Unpublished doctoral dissertation). Hofstra University, Hempstead, NY.

Stahl, S. A. (2002). Different strokes for different folks? In L. Abbeduto (Ed.), *Taking sides: Clashing on controversial issues in educational psychology* (pp. 98–107). Guilford , CT: McGraw-Hill.

Tschannen-Moran, M., & Hoy, W. K. (2000). A multidisciplinary analysis of the nature, meaning, and measurement of trust. *Review of Educational Research, 70,* 547–593.

White, E. B. (1952). *Charlotte's web.* New York: HarperCollins.

Index

CORWIN

A SAGE Company

The Corwin logo—a raven striding across an open book—represents the union of courage and learning. Corwin is committed to improving education for all learners by publishing books and other professional development resources for those serving the field of PreK–12 education. By providing practical, hands-on materials, Corwin continues to carry out the promise of its motto: **"Helping Educators Do Their Work Better."**